El anzuelo de Fenisa

862.3 Veg
Vega.
El anzuelo de Fenisa =
 Fenisa's hook, or, Fenisa.

**The Lorette Wilmot Library
Nazareth College of Rochester**

Lope de Vega

El anzuelo de Fenisa

Fenisa's Hook, or Fenisa the Hooker

Translated by David M. Gitlitz

For Linda, who has been partner all along the way

Trinity University Press gratefully acknowledges the assistance of the *Program for Cultural Cooperation Between Spain's Ministry of Culture and North American Universities* in making this publication possible.

Library of Congress Cataloging-in-Publication Data

```
Vega, Lope de, 1562-1635.
   Fenisa's hook (or Fenisa the hooker)

   Translation of: El anzuelo de Fenisa.
   I. Title.
PQ6439.A65E5  1988          862'.3           88-4887
ISBN 0-939980-19-3
```

The Spanish text of this edition was taken from *La Real Academia Española* (Madrid: Sucesores de Rivadaneyra, 1913), XIV, 483-526.

Art by Sandra French

Copyright © 1988 by David M. Gitlitz

Manufactured in the United States of America
Printed by Best Printing Company
Bound by Custom Bookbinders

Trinity University Press   715 Stadium Drive   San Antonio, Texas 78284

CONTENTS

Introduction: Lope de Vega and *Fenisa's Hook*   vii

Text and Translation of *El anzuelo de Fenisa*   1

INTRODUCTION: LOPE DE VEGA AND *FENISA'S HOOK*

The theater of Spain's seventeenth-century Golden Age, vast in scope, far-ranging in its sources, encyclopedic in its subject matter and its themes, has played an unjustly small part in the histories of world literature. The few plays well known to the modern reading public may in fact misrepresent the mainstream. Pedro Calderón de la Barca's wife murder plays *El pintor de su deshonra* [*The Painter of his Dishonor*] and *El médico de su honra* [*The Surgeon of his Honor*] and his philosophical masterpiece *La vida es sueño* [*Life is a Dream*] in their subject matter are atypical of his 120 extant plays, most of them romantic comedies. Tirso de Molina's *El burlador de Sevilla* [*Trickster of Seville*], the source for all later Don Juan plays, is very unlike the bulk of his work, again mostly comedy. Lope de Vega, best known perhaps for his two plays in which peasants overthrow a tyrannical nobleman (*Fuenteovejuna* and *Peribáñez*), wrote many dozens of other plays whose subjects are biblical, mythological, hagiographic, historical and pastoral, as well as hundreds of love comedies whose sources range from ancient history to the Italian *novella* to Lope's own love life.

Lope's little-known play *El anzuelo de Fenisa* [*Fenisa's Hook*], derived from tale VIII:10 of Boccaccio's *Decameron*, is worthy of our attention for a variety of reasons.[1] It is a sterling example of how Spanish playwrights adopted and modified their Italian Renaissance sources. It portrays the mercantile life that joined Spain to Italy in the seventeenth century and details the seamier side of Mediterranean port cities. The two principal women characters, the courtesan Fenisa and the scorned lover Dinarda, who dresses as a man to pursue her lover Albano, bring seventeenth-century concepts of gender roles sharply into focus. And beyond all this, *Fenisa's Hook* is a delightful comedy: intricately plotted, witty, with engaging characters and lyric verses, a good introduction to the mainstream comic theater of Spain's Golden Age.

I.

Lope de Vega was a man whose personal life and whose literary life were both so hyperbolic that they led his contemporary Cervantes to speak of him as "Nature's prodigy."[2] Madrid audiences of the early seventeenth century revered Lope as the creator of modern Spanish theater. His first biographer, Juan Pérez de Montalbán, estimated that between composing his first play at age twelve and his death sixty-one years later Lope had written more than eighteen hundred plays, all in metered, tightly rhymed verse, an average of one play every thirteen days! While modern literary historians set the total nearer eight hundred,[3] they still recognize Lope as the most prolific playwright of all time. Moreover, even if he had never written for the stage at all, his other works—poems, novels, epics—would still secure his place in the pantheon of talented authors of Spain's Golden Age.

Lope Félix de Vega Carpio[4] was born to tradesman parents in the boomtown atmosphere of Spain's new capital of Madrid[5] in 1562. He studied for a time with the Jesuits, served as a bishop's page in Avila, and began university studies in Alcalá de Henares. But his adolescent enthusiasm for life would not permit him to stay put for long: in a brief span of time he dropped out of the university, wandered in the north of Spain, sired the first of at least ten illegitimate children, enrolled at the University of Salamanca, enlisted in a naval expedition to the Azores, and then returned to Madrid. There, at age 21, he met the first great love of his life, the actress Elena Osorio, daughter of a prominent theatrical producer and wife of an actor in his troupe. Lope began a practice that he followed all his life: he turned his amorous affair into literature, spewing out ballads and plays in which his love and jealousy for Elena Osorio—thinly disguised under a variety of poetic names—and his scorn for various members of her family, were paraded before a Madrid public avid for details of their scandalous behavior. Elena's father sued Lope for libel, and early in 1588 Lope was arrested, imprisoned, and then banished from Madrid for four years.

Biographers all agree that Lope's poetic genius was lodged in a spirit given to passionate, impetuous, reckless behavior. No sooner had Lope been released from custody when, on the rebound from his affair with Elena Osorio, he fell in love with Isabel de Urbina, whose brother and father were prominent royal courtiers. He swept her away to Valencia, where she became pregnant, and then promptly left her to enlist as a marine in the so-called Invincible Armada that Philip II was sending against England. Lope survived the debacle, returning to Valencia with a newly composed epic poem in imitation of Ariosto. There, with his new wife and an innovative group of playwright colleagues, Lope began to write for the theater in earnest. Drawing on his military career, his university education and his knowledge of classical and Italian authors, he joined with his colleagues in attempts to adapt European theatrical traditions to the Spanish taste. Lope spent two productive years in Valencia before the need for a steady income led him into service with the Duke of Alba.

For the next decade Lope alternated between Madrid and Toledo while devoting himself with equal passion to women and to art. In 1595 his wife Isabel died giving birth to their second daughter. A brief affair with the widow Antonia Trillo led in 1596 to an indictment for concubinage. By 1598 he was living with Micaela Luján,[6] the wife of a traveling actor. By 1607, when it appears that Micaela had died, she had borne six children by one or another of the two men. This long-term, scandalous affair did not keep Lope from marrying, also in 1598, Juana de Guardo, daughter of a wealthy fish and meat merchant. For some years Lope managed two households, siring children in each, while churning out plays and poems in vast numbers.

By 1609 Lope had settled permanently in Madrid. In Madrid's theaters the steady flow of his dramatic production was winning the hearts of commoners and distressing the conservative critics who derided his plays for not adhering to the classical unities and for their blatant pandering to the taste of the rabble. Lope responded with a long poem, the *Arte nuevo de hacer comedias* [*New Art of Writing Plays*], endorsing with some reservations classical principles while at the same time ironically defending the theater's need to be able to adapt to changing times, and playwrights' need to please the public in order to make a living.

When in 1613 Juana de Guardo died in childbirth, Lope engaged briefly in a passionate affair with Jerónima de Burgos, whose attentions and money he accepted until her drinking and obesity drove him off. Now came a time of deep depression for Lope. A series of personal misfortunes—the deaths of Juana, Micaela, and his son Carlos, his near bankruptcy, and his subsequent rejection by the aristocracy—and his lifelong interest in religion and the church, led Lope in 1614 to profess a religious vocation. Atonement for his youthful profligacy would, he told the doubtful church fathers, govern his actions for the remainder of his days. Lope was ordained a priest in May of 1614. For a brief time he struggled to live a celibate Christian life; but it was not to be, for Lope soon became infatuated with yet another actress, Lucía de Salcedo, whom he referred to in his letters as the "madwoman." This tempestuous and unpleasant affair lasted only a short while, for then Lope fell in love with Marta de Nevares, a beautiful young woman, recently separated from her wife-beating husband. Though Lope's life with Marta was at first stormy, as the couple suffered attacks from both Lucía de Salcedo and Marta's husband Roque, before long Lucía desisted, and Roque died. Lope and Marta lived together for fifteen years with some of Lope's previous children, and some of their own. Not even Marta's blindness, which overtook her in 1622, nor her intermittent bouts of insanity, which lasted until her death in 1632, drove Lope from her.

Throughout these years Lope continued to write. At times his plays occupied the stages in every theater in Madrid. Other times the public seemed to reject his work. Yet Lope always came back with bursts of creativity that reestablished his primacy among playwrights of his day. But then a new series of personal misfortunes—Marta's death, the drowning death of his last male child, the abduction and later abandonment of his daughter Antonia Clara by a rake named Tenorio who ironically resembled Lope himself in his wilder days—drove him to fits of melancholy. Lope continued to pen comedies, but during these years he also wrote religious poems, a number of scathingly cynical plays, and even a mock-epic burlesque about cats. Disillusioned, repentant, adored by the public but bereft of both lovers and children, Lope died in 1635. His funeral cortege was the largest ever seen in Madrid.

II.

Lope inherited the rich cultural traditions of the sixteenth-century European Renaissance and transformed them with his artistic genius. Far ranging in his sources, his thematic interests, and his techniques, he hit upon a formula that was infinitely adaptable and appealing to both common and aristocratic tastes. While not every play followed the formula, the elements appear frequently enough to have created a coherent theatrical tradition, known to us now as the *comedia* , which flourished from 1600 to about 1680. In fact, a good working definition of a *comedia* is a play that adheres to Lope's formulation. Somewhat confusingly, the *comedia* is also used to refer to the entire corpus of seventeenth-century Spanish plays. These plays are written in three acts, each act of about one thousand verses.[7] The verse, generally in hendecasyllables (derived from Italian meters) or octosyllables (from the Spanish tradition), is arrayed in a number of conventional strophic forms, each tending to be used in certain kinds of situations: *romances* (ballads) for narration, sonnets for soliloquies, *redondillas* (quatrains rhyming *abba*) for romantic dialogue, and so forth. Lyric passages are interspersed, as are songs. Favorite themes are love and honor. The plays abound in local color. They mix characters from upper and lower classes. They frequently incorporate historical background, and they almost always develop multiple plots, which reinforce each other thematically.[8] Action tends to predominate over characterization; characters are revealed, and often tested, but rarely developed. There are numerous changes of scene, and the action takes place over several days (sometimes even years). Often a lower-class character, generally a servant, acts as *gracioso* (clown); humor is situational, visual, and verbal. Often tragic and comic elements are mixed. The ending is always "just," in the sense that it resolves conflicts in favor of the majoritarian values of Lope's day.[9] This formula equally well fits plots taken from a wide variety of sources: historic, folkloric, biblical, hagiographic, contemporary events, or the Italian novel.

Spaniards of the sixteenth and seventeenth centuries were avid consumers of Italian culture. For one thing, at that time the southern half of the Italian peninsula belonged to Spain; Naples and Palermo were Spanish ports. For another, adventurous Spanish youths often spent a few years in Italy in service with the army or the church. Literature by the Italian Renaissance masters was held in enormous prestige in Western Europe. The upper classes, well traveled in Italy, and solidly grounded in Latin as well as being native speakers of a closely related Romance language, had easy access to Italian literature in the original. The middle and lower classes provided a market for the burgeoning numbers of available translations. Ariosto's *Orlando furioso* was sold everywhere; Boccaccio's *Decameron*, to cite another example, first published in Spanish translation in Sevilla in 1496, had already been reprinted four times by 1550.[10] Not only were the Italians translated, of course, they were widely imitated throughout Europe.[11] To the Renaissance literary mind an author's originality lay not in the uniqueness of his subject matter, but rather in his treatment of that material. Albert Sloman reflected this ideal in commenting on Calderón's plot borrowings from earlier writers, when he said that imitations "need not compromise their integrity nor detract from their originality. Providing that the borrowing is imaginative, and that by the impact of their minds the appropriated material is transmuted, their work will be new and different and unique."[12] Under this principle, Renaissance authors appropriated at will plots, characters, situations, metaphors, and even rhetorical modes from sources as diverse as poems, plays and histories from classical antiquity, the Bible, and the works of the Italian masters.

Two factors were at work. One was the Renaissance dream, articulated by Herrera in his annotations to the poems of Garcilaso, to validate the quality and status of vernacular literature by imitating, equaling, and even besting classical and Italian models.[13] The other is that the voracious Spanish appetite for new plays drove playwrights to make rapid use of whatever source material they could find. Thus at some point in their careers nearly every Spanish writer imitated the Italians. Lope himself wrote long poems in imitation of Ariosto (*La hermosura de Angélica* [*The Beauty of Angelica*] – 1588?, published 1602) and Tasso (*Jerusalén conquistada* [*Jerusalem Regained*] – 1609). Toward the beginning of his career he also adapted plots of stories of Bandello, Boccaccio and Giraldi Cintio for his plays.[14] At least eight of Boccaccio's tales were brought to the stage by Lope's pen.[15]

The source for *Fenisa's Hook* is the tenth tale of the eighth day of the *Decameron*.[16] It will be useful to have some knowledge of Boccaccio's story in order to understand how Lope has structured his adaptation. Boccaccio's story is not only a classic *beffa*, the Italian term for an artful deceit or practical joke, but a double *beffa*, in which the trickster is in turn tricked by a variant of her own ruse, hoisted on her own petard.[17] In Boccaccio's tale a young Florentine woolen merchant, Niccol da Cignano, called Salabaetto, while registering his cargo in the customs house, is attracted to Madam Iancofiore. Boccaccio describes her profession as follows:

> There are many women, very fair of their person, but sworn enemies to honesty, who would be and are, by those who know them not, held great ladies and passing virtuous and who, being given not to shave, but altogether to flay men, no sooner espy a merchant there than they inform themselves by the book of the customs of that which he has there and what he is worth; after which, by their lovesome and engaging fashions and with the sweetest words, they study to allure the said merchants and draw them into the snare of their love.

Thus when Iancofiore learns the value of Salabaetto's goods, she feigns love for him and sets up an assignation in a bathhouse. In spite of this forward behavior, and her gifts to him of a ring, a girdle, a purse, and thirty ducats, he nevertheless believes she is a great lady. Once he has sold his goods for a handsome profit, Iancofiore invites him to dinner, inflames his passions with her attentions, and then by prior arrangement is called away. She returns weeping that unless she can pay one thousand florins in ransom in eight days her brother's head will be cut off. Salabaetto lends her five hundred. Immediately her attitude changes. She refuses to see him and refuses to repay the loan. Though the young man's eyes have been opened by her deceit, he decides not to press charges, because he had been forewarned and because he would leave himself open to ridicule. Instead he goes to Naples and plans a *contrabeffa*. He returns to Palermo with a cargo which, according to rumors he himself sets in motion, consists of fine clothing and oil worth two thousand florins. Iancofiore makes excuses: she behaved badly because she was upset, she did not get the money until after he had left, but now she will repay the five hundred and they will take up as before. But, alas!, Salabaetto learns that one of his ships has been taken by the corsairs of Monaco, and he must pay one thousand florins ransom. Unfortunately right now the market is low, so if he sells his warehoused goods he will take a loss. Iancofiore says that although she herself is strapped for cash, she knows of a moneylender—who turns out to be herself—who for only thirty percent interest, against a mortgage on the warehoused cargo, will lend him the money. Salabaetto, jubilant, takes the money and sails for Naples, where he "made merry for several days...over the cheat he had put upon the Sicilian trickstress." Iancofiore, puzzled when she does not hear from her lover for two months, has the chests forced open.

When she finds only seawater and cheap cloth she confesses herself outwitted.

Lope uses Boccaccio's entire story for the main plot of his play, changing only minor details.[18] In three places, however, he substantially improves on his source. Boccaccio's Iancofiore, for whom the story gives no biographical antecedents, is a cool professional. Passionate Fenisa was herself initially jilted by a lover, which is what motivates her to disdain and exploit men. Moreover, in spite of her professed immunity to affection, at the play's end Fenisa appears truly to have fallen in love with "Don Juan." Second, while Salabaetto was from the very first trusting of Iancofiore, Lucindo is suspicious of Fenisa. Moreover Lucindo's servant, Tristan, who like most *graciosos* in the *comedia* is a paragon of cynicism, repeatedly cautions his master against her. The result is to protract and introduce a note of tension into the schemes that Fenisa uses to separate Lucindo from his money. Last, in the *novella* it takes Iancofiore two months to discover she has been duped, but the play ends more neatly: Lucindo gloats as he sails away to Spain while Fenisa, opening the letter he has sent to disillusion her, precipitates the actions that rob her of her wealth and pride as the play comes to a close.

Lope's plays are almost invariably characterized by their dual or multiple plots, and his romantic comedies by the tangled nature of these plots. We are not surprised, therefore, when Lope interweaves with the Boccaccian tale several other stories which in the end become as important as the source story involving the courtesan Fenisa and her merchant lover Lucindo. To begin, Fenisa is also courted by two other men, Captain Osorio, a crusty old Spanish soldier who appears to be Fenisa's protector and pimp as well as her lover, and Albano, newly arrived from Spain, from where he has fled, having wounded a nobleman in a fight. Three other recent arrivals, Bernardo, Fabio and Dinarda, whom her companions believe to be a man, have come to Italy to improve on their penniless condition. Additionally Dinarda has come to pursue the man who has seduced and abandoned her, none other than Albano. The three decide that their best hope of success is to attract the attentions of "some high lady from Sicily" (v. 613), and for that purpose one will pretend to be a lord and the other two his servants. They cast lots, with the result that Dinarda is chosen lord and renamed "Don Juan de Lara." Taken by Captain Osorio to sup with Fenisa, "Don Juan" at once wins Fenisa's attention and the captain's unease.

Act II advances the Boccaccian tale to near completion while further entangling the subplots. Albano begins to suspect that "Don Juan" may be a woman, in fact the very woman he had loved back in Spain. When he interrogates the *gracioso* Fabio about this, Fabio bewilders him by replying, in a bastardized Italian, that perhaps Albano is a bit effeminate himself. Bernardo and Fabio also are intrigued by "Don Juan's" delicate appearance, and they too go about trying to discover if "he" is male or female. Meanwhile Fenisa, who up until now has cruelly exploited men, has truly fallen in love with "Don Juan," and Captain Osorio has become jealous.

Act III tangles the skein so much further that the story of Lucindo and Fenisa appears to recede to a second plane of importance. Bernardo and Fabio are now convinced that "Don Juan" is a woman. Albano, on the other hand, is now certain that "Don Juan" is not the woman he left behind in Spain. Lucindo reappears with his bogus trade goods accompanied by a new character, Dinarda's brother Don Félix, who has by now recovered from the wound Albano had given him, and who has come to Palermo to kill Albano. Captain Osorio, feeling himself neglected by Fenisa, has turned against her. "Don Juan," in a move to help the Captain take his vengeance, proposes marriage to Fenisa who, elated that she has fleeced Lucindo once again and has won "Don Juan's" hand, distributes gifts to everyone. Thus all is finally set for the climactic unravelling. Lucindo has set sail for Spain with Fenisa's money. Albano, who now knows that Don Félix has come to kill him, is delivering Lucindo's parting letter to Fenisa when Don Félix appears. "Don Juan" stops them from fighting, extracting a promise that they will put aside their grudge if "he" can produce Don Félix's sister Dinarda for Albano to marry. They agree, "Don Juan" changes roles, the assembled company marvel at the appearance of Dinarda, and domestic harmony is restored while Fenisa, deprived of both her capital and her intended husband, rages in despair.

III.

The multiple plots of *Fenisa's Hook* are tied together by an organizing principle which contrasts the mercantile values of the world of Fenisa and Lucindo with the aristocratic values of Albano, Félix and Dinarda. The commercial world, home to the characters of Boccaccio's *novella*, is a bustle of ships and customs sheds, merchants and courtesans, a world where wool and oils and sex and human affections are all coins of the realm. The second, the world of the nobility where honor and love presumably hold sway, is the conceptual rock upon which Spanish Golden Age *comedia* was built. The plays of Lope and his contemporaries routinely reaffirmed the preeminence of these values against all challengers.

At the same time cultures distant from this aristocratic milieu fascinated the Spanish Golden Age public. They avidly devoured the period's many picaresque novels[19] which depicted the colorful underworld of the Spanish cities, and the witty descriptive essays by people like Francisco de Quevedo[20] and Juan de Zabaleta[21] which detailed the underside of court life. People were intrigued with the details of the workings of these worlds. They consumed Cervantes's depictions of Monipodio's school for thieves in Seville[22] and Agustín de Rojas' descriptions of the economic misadventures of a traveling theater company.[23] The theater, too, was often a mirror of customs, depicting in minute detail everything from village festivals or military campaigns to the exotic locales of North Africa or Spain's overseas empire.[24] In this vein are the portraits in *Fenisa's Hook* of Palermo's contingent of foreign seamen, brokers, captains and courtesans. Lope's attention to detail, such as the minutiae of individual business transactions and mortgage terms, gives an aura of artistic verisimilitude to the portraiture.

Both Lucindo and Fenisa belong to the commercial world. Both are moved by a desire for personal gain. Both live by their wits, aided by their practical and often technical expertise about the workings of ships, ports, brokerage houses and the human passions. Both are confident of their own abilities. Each views the other, at least initially, as an easy opponent. But of the two Fenisa more clearly holds our attention. In the very title of the play it is clear that Lope has shifted the emphasis of Boccaccio's story from the merchant to the courtesan.[25]

Boccaccio characterized Iancofiore with two metaphors: she was a "barberess," "being given not to shave, but altogether to flay men," and also a huntress, ready to "draw them into the snare of...love."[26] Lope's Fenisa characterizes herself as an omnipotent fisherwoman. This concept dominates the play. Albano, who from the very first knows that Fenisa "gives up love for money with such ease" (v. 93), mocks her disdain, asking her, "Where will you sink your lovely hook/ to fish out a fat bulging purse?" (vv. 170-1) Fenisa angrily retorts that fishing is her destiny, her passion, and her trade:

> There was a star the day that I
> was born, a planet that inclined
> me to the sea, and there to try
> to look for fish, to fishes find,
> as others seek birds in the sky.
> . . . .
> I am driven by the same drive,
> but the shore is my hunting ground;

> that's why I came down here, to strive
> with my nets in the salty sound;
> that's how my star keeps me alive.
>   On this sweet lover's hook of mine
> the bait I use are eyes and tongue.
> Whoever nibbles at my twine,
> if he's foolish enough, and young,
> one year I play him on my line. (187-206)

The image of the "sweet lover's hook" appears some twenty times in the play, both in the speeches of her male opponents[27] and and in Fenisa's own self-definition.[28] She is so proud of her skill that, in a speech that sets the play's emblematic title firmly in our minds, she even invites Celia to emulate her:

Celia: Who can witness your artifice
and not feel great astonishment?

Fenisa: Hush. It's hardly anything. Look
at me, if you'd learn how to fish.
No finer lesson could you wish.
No one forgets Fenisa's hook! (1824-9)

The truth of such extravagant claims is borne out by Fenisa's actions. She is a master fisherwoman indeed, using a variety of stratagems to attract, hook, play and land her prey. When she trolls for Lucindo on the beach she flatters his good looks and his Spanish pride and claims that he has swept her off her feet. When she notes that he has shown his distrust of her by having deposited all his jewelry in safekeeping, she pretends to be disappointed in his lukewarm reaction to her, raising the specter that he has another love back in Valencia. She correctly deduces Lucindo's cash flow problem and obligates him to her with gifts. She correctly perceives that Lucindo's cynical servant Tristan is her enemy and astutely entangles him as well. Her promise of eroticism is far less blatant than Iancofiore's seduction of Salabaetto in a bathhouse (which is not surprising, given that Lope's work was written for the public stage), but it effectively whets Lucindo's appetite nonetheless. Fenisa first sends Celia to Lucindo's lodgings to see if his bed linens show the traces of another woman, and then feigns a fit of melancholy that draws Lucindo to her house where she can take advantage of his befuddled aroused state to strip him of his money. In the characters of Fenisa and Lucindo, Lope, himself well accustomed to the artifices of the amorous hunt, created a pair of skirmishers entirely believable in the psychological acuity with which they play one another.

But unlike Boccaccio's Iancofiore, Fenisa is motivated by something beyond naked acquisitiveness. In her youth she had been abandoned by the man she loved:

> Ever since the first man that I
> loved taught me the way to forget,
> in not loving I've become spry.
> One man got to me, and I get
> revenge on all men in reply. (122-6)

As Nancy D'Antuono astutely points out,
> denied recourse to satisfaction against the man who betrayed her, Fenisa's

anger and desire for vengeance is displaced toward all subsequent men who fall prey to her beauty. Contrary to her initial love encounter, the man is now the hapless victim, while Fenisa assumes the role of the faithless seducer, and relishes the power which the turnabout affords.[29]

Fenisa claims other motives as well: once she has attained the free life of an independent woman, she cannot bear to give it up (vv. 139-41). Moreover, she asserts that she is a sort of moral scourge for men who have been deprived of their rational facility by women's beauty (vv. 142-4). Yet it is clear that these are very secondary motivations and that Fenisa is really driven by cupidity, vengeance and her desire to exert power over men. Lope, through Lucindo, is an acute observer when he hints that to find satisfaction with men Fenisa must either abuse or be abused, and that barring this, she is most likely to be attracted to another woman:

> for the only type her kind can
> love is a woman, or a man
> who mistreats her...(2371-3)

This propensity explains Fenisa's attraction to the delicate "Don Juan" and sharpens the embarrassment and ridicule which she suffers at the play's end.

In Lope's male-dominated world, women could only find legitimate fulfillment in their roles vis-à-vis men, as wives and mothers. It is true that many contemporary fictional works deal with assertive women: female bandits, learned women, amazons and a wide variety of *mujeres esquivas* (women who are opposed to marriage). Yet, as Melveena McKendrick has noted, in every case their defiance is "directed against the natural order of things as decreed by God."[30] Lope himself is unequivocally clear about this. In the dedication of one of his plays he states: "It is vanity in a woman to despise men, for when Aristotle said that women desire men the way matter desires form he realized that he was saying no small thing."[31] In Lope's ethos poetic justice demands that a disdainful woman be given her comeuppance, and it is for this reason that at the play's end Fenisa has to be doubly deceived, deprived of both of the things she holds most dear: her faith in her business acumen and her pride in her emotional self-sufficiency. She has lost her capital to Lucindo's wily mirroring of her deceitful stratagems. And her much touted freedom (vv. 139-41) and disdain for men turn to ashes when she loses her heart to "Don Juan" only to learn that her lover is a woman in disguise. Poetic justice has been done. Although none of the characters are wholly blameless, Fenisa's values are the most questionable of the lot. The rough treatment of Fenisa at the conclusion may offend some modern sensibilities, but it is clear that Lope meant for us to laugh at Fenisa, not to cry with her.

The handsome young merchant Lucindo is a worthy opponent for Fenisa, although his professional sagacity is undermined by his youth and his inexperience in amorous matters.[32] From his opening moment Lucindo is predisposed to be wary, recognizing that women are

> ...the worst enemy of trade.
>   Neither debt nor insolvency,
> nor broken trust nor broken wills,
> neither bad credit nor bankruptcy,
> nor debtor's death with unpaid bills,
> not even wild tempests at sea
>   are a fraction as bad as when
> a merchant throws himself at love. (291-8)

His first words to Fenisa ring with the hollow gallantry of a conventional opening lover's gambit (vv. 339-41); when she replies in kind, however, his good sense tells him to back off: "I hear you, but I'm still unsure / somehow.... Don't you think I should be/ wary? I am a stranger here" (vv. 394-8). Tristan, Lucindo's servant, continually warns him that Fenisa is a commercial woman of the worst sort (vv. 453-74), yet Lucindo, perhaps overreacting to Tristan's cynicism, is prepared to believe the best:

> ...It could be the case
> that she's a well-born maid, a dame
> most illustrious in this place. (479-81)

Deception and self-deception are intertwined. From the very start Lope has imbued Lucindo with a realistic ambivalence toward Fenisa, a vacillating attitude that remains until Lucindo finds himself fleeced toward the end of the second act.

Lope makes clear that Lucindo is a merchant, not an aristocrat. Although he courts Fenisa with cliché metaphors that are common to Golden Age upper-class literary upper-class lovers, he also links this language to his familiar commercial world: for example, wishing that each element of his ship were precious jewels that he could give to her (vv. 945-67). Although he may employ the language of the higher emotions, in the last analysis in Lucindo's world love, or at least sex, is a commodity. The gulf that purportedly separates Lucindo's world from that of the protagonists of the play's second plot is made explicit in a shipboard conversation in Act III between Lucindo and Dinarda's brother Félix:

> Lucindo: ...You've greatly honored me
> by not treating me shabbily
> or taking my low birth for ill.
>   Even though you, Don Félix, are
> a *caballero* from Seville,
> I a Valencian merchant...(2327-32)

The friendship that Don Félix offers is taken fawningly as a courtesy by Lucindo, a man who will never be able to append an aristocratic "Don" to his own name. Although some class ascension was possible in Spain's Golden Age, since new wealth sometimes could be used to purchase estates, and for some people, as Pike makes clear, the merchant state became "an intermediary stage in the social hierarchy to be abandoned as soon as possible,"[33] nevertheless the *comedia* did not express approval of such practice. While *Fenisa's Hook* does not overtly condemn Lucindo's values, on the whole the Spanish *comedia* not only despised the commercial class, but avoided presenting in positive light the bourgeois virtues of economic prudence, saving or hard work.[34] Lucindo is not apologetic about his values; in fact he prizes his capital investment the way aristocrats prize their personal honor, for possessions are equated to a good name:

> ...for a merchant honor lies
> in his merchandise, his business.
>   For once you lose your capital
> you lose your credit too, and then...(2424-7)

The differences between Lucindo and Albano are made clear by their opposite approaches to the affronts they have received. Lucindo, having been cheated, will in turn cheat. Albano, having been wounded in a fight, will seek redress with sword in hand.

Lucindo's lack of nobility stands out when he urges Albano to caution and hints that he engage in foul play:

> If you plan to take sword to that man who
> caused you such offense, please let me assure
> you, there is a better way...(2666-8)

Although Lucindo has suffered, none of his concerns are in any way transcendent, and this explains in part why the play's focus shifts in the third act from the story of Lucindo and Fenisa to that of Albano and Dinarda.[35]

The play's most engaging character may well be Dinarda, the abandoned lover who dons men's clothing as she goes to Italy to seek her fortune, to escape her shame and, incidentally, to recapture her lost lover Albano. When we first meet her on the beach in Palermo with her two traveling companions, Fabio and Bernardo, they are penniless. Of the three Dinarda is the most assertive: they would be servants, while she prefers soldiering (v. 548). When by lot she is chosen leader, they readily assume the servants' roles. It is clear that they do not know that she is a woman.

The audience, of course, does know, for the stage directions indicate that Dinarda is dressed in men's travel clothing, a short doublet and form-fitting hose. Women of Lope's time wore voluminous long dresses which securely covered up everything that might indicate their true shapes. Men wore sheer stockings and short breeches that left little to the imagination. This, in part, explains the popularity in the Golden Age theater of the female disguise plot. There were hundreds of plays in which women disguised as men took the roles of pages, soldiers, bandits and students.[36] Moralists of the day were unrelenting in their condemnation of the convention. To cite just two examples, Fray José de Jesús María in 1598 called it a "lascivious practice designed to fire hearts with fatal concupiscence," and Juan de Mariana some years later called it a "maximum perversity."[37]

In spite of one or two examples to the contrary, we can assume that women did not walk the streets of Spain dressed as men.[38] Nonetheless, the disguise plot served important theatrical purposes. The first might be termed the need for titillation: presumably a certain number of people flocked to the theater then as now to see revealed there what was elsewhere hidden to view.[39] The second was the convenience of the disguise device in the shaping of plot. As Victor O. Freeburg pointed out in his classic discussion of disguise plots, "disguise is an effective dramatic contrivance because the deception which produces action and the recognition which ends it are fundamentally dramatic transactions;...a device which complicates and is at the same time capable of resolving is especially desirable."[40] In *Fenisa's Hook* Dinarda's disguise drives the curiosity of Fabio, Bernardo and Albano, it leads Captain Osorio to seek to use "Don Juan" as an ally in taking vengeance on Fenisa, and it precipitates the second of the two ways in which Fenisa is deceived and brought low. All of these plot threads and two additional ones—Don Félix's seeking the man who wounded him in Spain, and Albano's abandonment of his former lover—are unraveled in the last scene when Dinarda reveals her true self.

IV.

In few areas did the values of Lope's day differ more completely from our own than in attitudes toward sex and gender roles. Modern audiences may find strange the fact that Fenisa is condemned for her greed, her presumptuous reliance on her wit and her disdain of love, but never for her sexual license. Or that Albano, already presumably in love back in Spain, is not censured for his attentions to Fenisa or his abandonment of Dinarda. Or that Captain Osorio, Fenisa's protector and procurer, is portrayed positively. Or that Dinarda so readily takes leave of her home and her reputation to pursue her lover to Italy, or that she adopts men's clothing for that purpose. Yet none of these stage behaviors would have raised eyebrows of theatergoers of Lope's day and none would have provoked controversy except with the moralists who railed against the male disguise.

For most moral philosophers of the period, women were daughters of Eve, agents of the devil, both tempting and easily tempted in matters of the flesh. Lope subscribed to the Aristotelian doctrine that women were imperfect and imperfectible,[41] and that men's and women's roles were sharply defined. Men worked, governed, administered; men took care of women; and men might take their pleasures where they pleased. Women bore children.[42] God created women to be men's helpmates; men were women's first cause and final end, and marriage was their birthright.[43] Lope agreed with the prevailing attitude that women served three purposes for men: to receive the noble aspirations of their loving hearts, to service their lustful enthusiasms, and to bear and rear their children and manage their houses. Where twentieth-century Western sensibilities tend to conflate these roles into one, seventeenth-century men did not. Where, at least in most of Europe in the 1980s, codes of chastity are presupposed to apply equally to men and to women, in Lope's day the double standard was the norm. Men could sow wild oats without incurring censure. In literature they were rarely called directly to task for seducing and abandoning young virgins.[44] Women were expected to remain chaste until marriage, but if they did not, moral convention dictated that once a woman had had intercourse with a man, that man was her only possible marriage partner. Even if he had abandoned her, even if he was a rake or a scoundrel, if at any point he offered her marriage she accepted. As Melveena McKendrick points out, abandoned women accepted "marriage as satisfaction for this treatment because for them marriage is the only real satisfaction. In the seventeenth century the jilted woman was an unmarketable commodity."[45] In literary works of the sort that lead to a happy ending, the abandoned woman routinely donned men's clothing in order to pursue her lover and secure through marriage a legitimized, productive future for herself. In real life a woman who did not want to or could not marry had few other choices: she could remain with her family, or become a *dueña* (governess), a nun or a prostitute or bawd.

In Spain prostitutes were lambasted from the pulpits, but largely as transmitters of disease. They were widely recognized as a necessary evil since men were seen as lustful creatures. Unless society provided an acceptable way for them to vent their lust, their own decent wives and daughters would not be safe. Prostitution flourished in every major European city. By the middle of the seventeenth century Madrid had eight hundred licensed brothels.[46] Seville, in addition to some three thousand streetwalkers,[47] had an entire district, the Arenal, reserved for strictly licensed and controlled brothels.[48] Prostitutes ranged in status from the lowly streetwalkers, to women who worked in brothels, or kept brothels, to courtesans who adopted many of the demeanors of the aristocracy and sometimes bordered on being kept women.[49] In the moral literature of the time, common prostitutes were seen as fallen or lost women. More generally, women were held to be "daughters of Eve," always just a step away from whoredom. They were usually considered frail of will and uncontrolled in their carnal desires: thus the locked doors, fettering clothing and protocol, and the omnipresent chaperone or *dueña*. For some authors women were little more than allegorized lustful embodiments of lechery, broadly representing post-lapsarian human nature or, in the case of courtesans and their courtly clients, narrowly representing the *urbs* as cesspool, the court as the corrupt essence of all that is wrong with government, the triumph of lust and greed over reason and public spirited selflessness. This is not the case for Lope who, unlike many of his Spanish or Elizabethan counterparts,[50] was not often given to sermonizing on the stage.

Among prostitutes a subgroup, to which Fenisa clearly belongs, is the *buscona* (con artist) who does not charge directly for sex but who uses her sexuality and her wits to separate her client-victim from his possessions.[51] In literature these women are routinely praised for their cleverness, and almost as routinely outwitted by their intended victims. *Busconas* in literature are not censured for their sensuality. Rather, the power that their eroticism gives them over men is portrayed as one more weapon in the arsenal of befuddlement. This is how Lope portrays Fenisa. She is not an evil allegorical figure, but rather a human being of mixed character and dubious morals, sympathetic and abrasive by turns, whose fault is that she is doubly presumptive: she thinks that she can outwit the Valencian merchant Lucindo, and that she herself is immune from the effects of erotic attraction.

Gender, and its relation to the sources and uses of power, is a theme latent in much of the literature of the period. Lope's society openly acknowledged that men were empowered by their gender, that within the constraints of honor and station they were free to act as they please. Just as well accepted was the fact that the constraints placed on women were more restrictive, that women too were free to act, but only within their narrowly circumscribed roles. In literature the possibility of women's distancing themselves from the male-dominated world did exist, but the so-called *mujeres esquivas* (reluctant brides) were deemed aberrant, and were generally reconciled in the end to their traditional roles vis-à-vis men. Moreover, even while rejecting men they had not succeeded in redefining the traditional roles; in fact their rejection of the societal norms only insured their impotence. In order to take an assertive role in society, in literature women were forced to adopt male characteristics, to become what the period called *mujeres varoniles*, a term which, defined as it was by the male-dominated value system, carried no negative connotations.[52] In literature one key strategy for attaining the power of freedom of action was to adopt male attire. While female fashion of the period was designed to cover up the female form, and to hamper freedom of movement, male dress facilitated movement.[53] On stage scanty male tights and short breeches instantly revealed that the wearer was a woman, yet convention dictated that this be ignored, so that while the audience was aware of the disguised woman's true sex the other characters routinely assumed her to be a male. The disguise enabled the female to act in situations where she normally would be at great physical risk.

If acting male-ly as a *mujer viril* was one source of power, money was another. Although clad with negative connotations in the literature of the period for reasons that have been discussed, in real life the power of money often prevailed. Successful commerce was a source of power. Prostitutes, of course, were objects of commerce and thus not empowered, even by their sexual attractiveness. Women of Fenisa's sort, not exactly courtesans but perhaps the dockside equivalent, were both objects and agents of commerce, combining the roles of whore and bawd. As agents they joined the "man's world of the manipulation of money and power."[54] The freedom of movement they enjoyed was that of the merchant. It is as merchant to merchant that Fenisa engages Lucindo, and when she loses, it is because Lucindo has outsmarted her on a business deal. The outcome is foreordained, however, because although Fenisa tries to behave as if she were a merchant of status equal to that of her male adversary, Lope shows us that at heart she is an emotional woman. She gains temporary advantage when she uses her erotic attraction to cloud Lucindo's judgment, but he defeats her when she loses her head (i.e., her business acumen) to an infatuation that, founded as it is on her and Lucindo's deceitful intentions, is doomed to failure. This emotion is not love, in the sense that Dinarda and Albano love, because it is always tainted with the base motives of commerce.

For modern sensibilities not so finely attuned to the implications of class distinctions as were the audiences of Lope's day, the world of this play may seem cruel. We perceive little difference in the behavior of Dinarda and Albano on the one hand and of Fenisa and Lucindo on the other. If Fenisa would use her sexual attractiveness to overpower Lucindo in order to fleece him of his goods, so too would Dinarda and her companions deceive some rich Sicilian lady for their personal gain (v. 613). Fenisa, seduced and abandoned, turns sour and vengeful. Albano, seducer and abandoner, is rewarded in the end with marriage to Dinarda. Although Fenisa and Lucindo, and perhaps Dinarda and her companions too, are all merchants in the world of sex, only Fenisa is punished. The universe in which they live, where sex is a basis of commerce and the higher emotions are attenuated by the motives and actions of their possessors, for all its exoticism seems to us bleak and dehumanized.

Yet in the theater of Lope's day what resolved these potentially troublesome conflicts of gender definition was the unifying philosophical principle that held that true love was the supreme power, the true monarch. Love might temporarily cloud its subjects' powers of rational thought, and cause them to do things which in any other context would be unacceptably scandalous or cruel. But the actions of Dinarda, and ultimately of Albano too, are acceptable to Lope's audience because the two of them are moved by the power of love. Their love, as compromised and as lacking in passion or sincerity as it may seem to us today, is superior and ultimately successful because it is rooted in the approved values of the era. We admire and laugh at the wily schemes of Fenisa and Lucindo, but because they are not legitimately governed by this supreme human passion, we are not forgiving of them, and ultimately we are led to condemn their behavior. But Dinarda lives in a fantasy world, the escapist world of the theater, of wish fulfillment brought alive on the stage, where a woman dressed as a man could move freely in hostile environments, where parted lovers could be neatly reunited at the drop of a disguise, and where love triumphs in the end.

V.

Plays of the Golden Age were written in verse, and playwrights of the period had to learn to manage with ease a wide variety of complex metrical forms. Some scenes, particularly those featuring characters of ponderous importance, would use hendecasyllables, a popular eleven-syllabled Renaissance meter of Italian origin which, in the theater, was most often cast into sonnets (commonly rhyming ABBA,ABBA,CDE,CDE[55]), octaves (ABABABCC), chain rhymed tercets (ABA,BCB,CDC, etc), or in blocks of unrhymed verses. Sonnets were most often used for soliloquies (as in the matched pair that close Act II of *Fenisa's Hook*), while the other stanzas accommodated both formal speeches and ordinary dialogue. Nevertheless the most common meter was the traditional Spanish octosyllable, which could appear in a variety of stanzas. One, the *romance* (ballad), featured assonant rhyme in every second verse; *romances* were the preferred meter for narrating background events (as in vv. 1275-1412), although they could also be used for ordinary dialogue (vv. 3098-3232). The most common octosyllabic stanza was the *redondilla* (quatrain: rhyming *abba*), used in this play in fifty percent of the verses. The second most common was the *quintilla* (a five-lined stanza generally rhyming *ababa*), used in twenty-six percent of the play's verses. Plays generally ran to three thousand or three thousand two hundred verses (approximately two hours in playing time), and whether Lope composed one every two weeks or only one a month, he had to be quick and accurate with his versifying. Modern critics are awed to find *comedias* as perfectly formed as they generally are; it is rare to find a play with more than the two stanzaic errors that occur in *Fenisa's Hook*.[56]

Most modern translations of *comedias* are rendered into prose, which I believe deprives them of several elements crucial to the original. For one thing, rhyme and rhythm provided mnemonic crutches for the actors, who often had to learn parts in a great rush. For another, the casting of formal speeches such as soliloquies into complex stanzas like sonnets created in the ears of the more discerning members of the audience a sense of impending completeness that heightened the tension inherent in the content of the speech. But perhaps more importantly, when one speaks of ordinary things while using highly artificial rhythmic and rhyming structures, one employs a rhetorically intensified mode of speech in which ordinary language ceases to be ordinary. One of the reasons that the *comedias* created such an effective fantasy world was that the plays' versification separated stage speech from that of everyday reality. The closer the modern translator can come to this original rhetorical mode, the more accurate and enriching will be the experience for the audience.

Besides, translating Lope into verse is hard, and that makes it fun and worth doing for its own sake. I have tried to stay very close to the metrical conventions of the original. My only innovation, if it may be called that, was to use two separate rhyme schemes for the *romance* meter: the long narrative in Act II is cast into ballad quatrains, quite regular in meter and consonantly rhymed in the second and fourth lines which creates, I think, a pattern clearly recognized as "poetic" to the modern American ear and sets these verses off from the less rhythmic language which surrounds them. For the other *romance* passage, devoted to dialogue, I kept the ballad rhythm but mirrored the Spanish use of assonant rhyme. Tristan's sonnet at the end of the second act concludes with an "-*ato*" rhyme that is particularly inelegant to the Spanish ear. I tried to achieve this in English with a staccato rhythm and lots of monosyllabic rhyme words ending in "t."

The most troublesome passages to translate are those which play with language. This *comedia*'s most salient example is the tangle of concepts associated with "cats" in Act II. Fenisa is a "cat," the coins repose in a "cat-purse," and the money which changes hands is referred to as a "kitty."[57] A second difficulty comes with allusive language when the allusions are not readily available to the modern audience. Since footnotes do not play well on the stage, I have from time to time tried to clarify or simplify an allusion in the text itself. A third challenge came with the macaronic Italian spoken by Fabio in Act II. Spanish audiences, native speakers of a language closely related to Italian, would have picked up the overall sense of Fabio's jests, if not every word. For English-speaking audiences I have tried to create a patois which is half-English, half-Italian, strange enough to provoke laughter while clear enough to communicate sense. Whatever success this and the whole of my labors may have can only be proved in the playing.

Fenisa's Hook: Metrical Structures

	Verses	Spanish Meter	English Meter
I.	1-106	tercetos encadenados	chain-rhymed tercets
	107-531	quintillas	octosyllabic stanzas: ababa
	532-1047	redondillas	octosyllabic stanzas: abba
II.	1048-1262	quintillas	octosyllabic stanzas: varied rhyme
	1263-1274	redondillas	octosyllabic stanzas: abba
	1275-1412	romance: ó-a	ballad meter: couplets
	1413-1476	redondillas	octosyllabic stanzas: abba
	1477-1486	canción	song
	1487-1554	redondillas	octosyllabic stanzas: abba
	1555-1568	soneto	sonnet
	1569-1641	endecasílabos sueltos	rhymed pentameter
	1642-1869	redondillas	octosyllabic stanzas: abba
	1870-1925	octavas reales	octaves: ABABABCC
	1926-2081	redondillas	octosyllabic stanzas: abba
	2082-2109	soneto	sonnets
III.	2110-2245	redondillas	octosyllabic stanzas: abba
	2246-2305	endecasílabos sueltos	unrhymed pentameter
	2306-2661	redondillas	octosyllabic stanzas: abba
	2662-2725	octavas reales	octaves: ABABABCC
	2726-2776	endecasílabos sueltos	unrhymed pentameter
	2777-2790	soneto	sonnet
	2791-3005	quintillas	octosyllabic stanzas: varied rhyme
	3006-3097	redondillas	octosyllabic stanzas: abba
	3098-3233	romance: í-a	ballad meter: assonance ee

Notes

[1] *Fenisa's Hook* was first published in 1617 in *Parte VIII* of Lope's plays. According to S. Griswold Morley and Courtney Bruerton, it was most likely written between 1604 and 1606: *Cronología de las comedias de Lope de Vega* (Madrid: Gredos, 1968), p. 282. The play is available in Spanish in three modern editions: that of La Real Academia Española (Madrid: Sucesores de Rivadaneyra, 1913), XIV, 483-526, from which the text of my edition is taken; that in the *Comedias escogidas de Frey Lope Félix de Vega Carpio* (Madrid: Biblioteca de Autores Españoles, 1950), III, 363-86; and that of Federico Carlos Sainz de Robles, *Obras escogidas de Lope Félix de Vega Carpio* (Madrid: Aguilar, 1958), I, 886-924. The play has also been adapted four times by subjecting it to a variety of excisions. The first, a reworking by Cándido María Trigueros, was published separately as a *comedia suelta* under the title *La buscona* (Madrid: Librería González, 1803). The second, by Cristóbal de Castro, featuring very explicit stage directions (Madrid: Sociedad de Autores Españoles, 1912), was directed in the Teatro Español in Madrid by the novelist Benito Pérez Galdós. The third, by Cándido Maizal, whose text I have been unable to locate, is referred to in an article by José Luis Alonso in *Acento cultural*, 12-13 (1961), p. 119. The fourth, by Juan-Germán Schroeder, was produced in the Teatro María Guerrero in 1961 and is reviewed in the issue of *Acento cultural* cited above. Professor Anita Stoll has in progress a study of these reworkings or *refundiciones*. *Fenisa's Hook* has not been previously translated into English.

[2] Cervantes, in the prologue to his *Ocho comedias y ocho entremeses* [*Eight Plays and Eight Interludes*] (1615), says that "Nature's prodigy, great Lope de Vega, ran away with the monarchy of the stage" ("el monstruo de la naturaleza, el gran Lope de Vega, alzóse con la monarquía cómica").

[3] For a brief summary of the controversy over how many plays Lope actually wrote, see Francis C. Hayes, *Lope de Vega* (New York: Twayne, 1967), pp. 75-77.

[4] The best biography of Lope de Vega in English is still Hugo A. Rennert's *The Life of Lope de Vega (1562-1635)* (Glasgow: 1904; reprinted by G. E. Stechert and Company, New York: 1937). An easily available biography can be found in Hayes, pp. 17-41. Perhaps the most readable brief biography is in the introduction to Michael McGaha's edition of Lope's *Lo fingido verdadero* [*Acting is Believing*] (San Antonio: Trinity University Press, 1986), pp. 3-21.

[5] The court traveled with the king until Philip II, eschewing any of Spain's large and politically complex cities, chose as his capital in 1561 the village of Madrid.

[6] Nancy D'Antuono has argued convincingly that *Fenisa's Hook*, written toward the end of Lope's affair with Micaela Luján, is directly inspired by their relationship and that "both Albano and Lucindo represent Lope; the former only in the initial portions of the comedy, the latter as the literary projection of a youthful adventure." *Boccaccio's "Novelle" in the Theater of Lope de Vega* (Madrid: José Porrúa Turanzas, 1983), p. 114.

[7] My discussion here is influenced by that of Hayes, pp. 79-80.

[8] A good overview of the structure and function of multiple plot plays is that of Richard Levin, *The Multiple Plot in English Renaissance Drama* (Chicago: University of Chicago Press, 1971).

[9] A. A. Parker, "The Approach to the Spanish Drama of the Golden Age," *Tulane Drama Review*, IV (1959), pp. 42-59.

[10] Caroline B. Bourland, *The Short Story in Spain in the Seventeenth Century* (Northampton, Massachusetts: Smith College, 1927), p. 55, n. 12.

[11] See the extensive list compiled by Florence Nightingale Jones, *Boccaccio and his Imitators* (Chicago: University of Chicago Press, 1910).

[12] Albert Sloman, *The Dramatic Craftsmanship of Calderón* (Oxford: The Dolphin

Book Company, 1969), p. 9.

[13] *Garcilaso de la Vega y sus comentaristas*, ed. Antonio Gallego Morell (Madrid: Gredos, 1972), pp. 311, 340.

[14] Raymond Lewis Scungio, *A Study of Lope de Vega's Use of Italian "Novelle" as Source Material for his Plays*, Ph.D. diss., Brown University, 1961, p. 193.

[15] D'Antuono, p. xi. These plays are: *La boda entre dos maridos* (1595-1601), *El halcón de Federico* (1601-5), *El ejemplo de casadas y prueba de la paciencia* (1599-1603), *El anzuelo de Fenisa* (1604-6), *El servir con mala estrella* (1604-6), *El llegar en ocasión* (1605-8), *La discreta enamorada* (1606), and *El ruiseñor de Sevilla* (1603-8).

[16] Giovanni Boccaccio, *Decameron*, The John Payne Translation revised and annotated by Charles S. Singleton (Berkeley: University of California Press, 1982), Vol. II, pp. 633-47. All quotations are from this edition.

[17] The double *beffa* abounds in the literature of Spain's Golden Age, appearing in everything from picaresque novels (such as in *Lazarillo de Tormes*, when Lazaro induces the blind man, who had bashed Lazaro's head against a stone bull on the bridge in Salamanca, into jumping face first into a stone pillar; or in Cervantes' *El casamiento engañoso* [*The Deceitful Marriage*], where the conniving bridegroom, who wants only his intended's money, is instead both fleeced and poxed by her) to serious religious drama (such as Tirso's *Burlador de Sevilla* [*Trickster of Seville*] when the trickster, who has seduced so many women by falsely offering them his hand, is dragged off to hell by the falsely proffered hand of the Comendador's statue).

[18] Salabaetto is sent to Palermo by his masters; Lucindo by his father. Iancofiore gives Salabaetto gifts; Fenisa also lends Lucindo money. Iancofiore introduces the story about her captive brother in the middle of lovemaking with Salabaetto; Fenisa has refused to see Lucindo, and when he at last enters her house, she appears in mourning. It takes Salabaetto two weeks to discover he has been tricked; Lucindo realizes this immediately, when he is refused entrance to Fenisa's house at the end of the second act. In the play Lucindo concludes the *contrabeffa* by writing Fenisa a letter; in Boccaccio's story Iancofiore does not learn she has been duped until she has the chests forced open two months later.

[19] Some principal works of the genre contemporary with Lope are: Mateo Alemán, *Guzmán de Alfarache* (1599, 1604), translated by James Mabbe as *The Rogue, or The Life of Guzmán de Alfarache* (London: 1622), ed. James Fitzmaurice-Kelly (London: Constable, 1924; reprint New York: AMS Press, 1967); Francisco López de Ubeda, *La pícara Justina* (1605); Vicente Espinel, *La vida del escudero Marcos de Obregón* (1618); Jerónimo de Alcalá Yáñez, *El donado hablador* (1624, 1626); Francisco de Quevedo, *El buscón* (1626), translated by Charles Duff as *The Life of the Great Rascal* in *Quevedo: The Choice Humorous Works* (London: Routledge; New York: Dutton, 1926) and by Hugh A. Harter as *The Scavenger* (New York: Las Américas, 1962); Alonso de Castillo Solórzano, *La niña de los embustes* (1632), *La garduña de Sevilla* (1634), *El bachiller Trapaza* (1634); Luis Vélez de Guevara, *El diablo cojuelo* (1641).

[20] In the 1620's Quevedo published a number of satirical descriptive fictional works, most written two decades earlier, including *Premática y aranceles generales*, *Cartas del caballero de la Tenaza*, and his masterful collection *Los sueños*, translated by Charles Duff as *The Visions*, in *Quevedo: The Choice Humorous Works*.

[21] Juan de Zabaleta, *Día de fiesta por la mañana* (1654) *y por la tarde* (1659).

[22] Miguel de Cervantes Saavedra, *Rinconete y Cortadillo* (1613).

[23] Agustín de Rojas, *El viaje entretenido* (1603).

[24] Plays of this sort are legion. Some examples from Lope's theater are *La noche de San Juan* (1631), *La Santa Liga* (1595-1603), *El Argel fingido* (1599) and *El Brasil restituido* (1625).

[25] Scungio, p. 134.

²⁶ *Decameron*, p. 634.

²⁷ Osorio: "She is an expert in the art / of fishing foreign purses" (2678-9); Lucindo: "The hook that she uses to catch / men is to give them gifts" (2374-5); Tristan: "She's down here with bait on her hook" (490). See also verses 1120, 2082, 2614, 2776, 2981, 3097.

²⁸ "Now there's a handsome visitor! / Think he's a good fish for my hook?" (327-8); "With my tricks I'm / certain to fish up all his cash." (430-1); "His lordship gobbled up the bait." (1819). See also verses 751, 850, 3031.

²⁹ D'Antuono, p. 115.

³⁰ Melveena McKendrick, "Women Against Wedlock: The Reluctant Brides of Golden Age Drama," in Beth Miller, ed., *Women in Hispanic Literature: Icons and Fallen Idols* (Berkeley: University of California Press, 1983), p. 116.

³¹ "Vanidad es en una mujer despreciar los hombres, pues cuando Aristóteles dijo que la mujer le apetecía como la materia a la forma no pensó que era pequeño el encarecimiento." From the dedication to *La vengadora de las mujeres* [*The Woman Who Avenged Women*], quoted by Melveena McKendrick, *Woman and Society in the Spanish Drama of the Golden Age: A Study of the* Mujer varonil (Cambridge: Cambridge University Press, 1974), p. 117.

³² D'Antuono, p. 116. Charles Dejob points out that the "prudenza mercantile...nel giovine si mischia all'imprudenza della sua età." "La 10a. Novella dell'ottava Giornata del *Decameron* e *El anzuelo de Fenisa* di Lope de Vega," *Rassegna Bibliografica della Letteratura Italiana I* (1893), p. 150.

³³ Ruth Pike, *Aristocrats and Traders: Sevillian Society in the Sixteenth Century* (Ithaca: Cornell University Press, 1972), p. 100. The purchase of noble rank was a strategy often used in the sixteenth century by prominent new-Christian families, recently converted from Judaism, with the result that the practice reaped a double dose of scorn both from the traditional aristocracy and from the old-Christian peasantry.

³⁴ José María Díez Borque, *Sociología de la comedia española del siglo XVII* (Madrid: Cátedra, 1976), p. 228.

³⁵ D'Antuono, p. 122.

³⁶ Carmen Bravo-Villasante, *La mujer vestida de hombre en el teatro español* (Madrid: Revista de Occidente, 1955). She lists by title 109 plays by Lope de Vega alone which include women dressed as men (pp. 21-4). See also B. B. Ashcom, "Concerning 'La mujer en hábito de hombre' in the *Comedia*," *Hispanic Review* 28 (1960), pp. 43-62.

³⁷ Bravo-Villasante, p. 209, 212.

³⁸ McKendrick cites the case of the actress Barbara Coronel, who affected men's clothing offstage as well as on. *Woman and Society*, p. 42. Mary Elizabeth Perry recounts the famous case of a Basque nun who, disguised as a man, worked in Mexico for twenty years before revealing herself as a woman in order to escape hanging. *Crime and Society in Early Modern Seville* (Hanover: Dartmouth Press, 1980), p. 216.

³⁹ McKendrick, *Woman and Society*, p. 321. For Díez Borque, in all of the theater the male disguise was "el máximo placer erótico que se le brindaba al espectador" (*Sociología de la comedia*, p. 47). See also David M. Gitlitz, "*El Galán Castrucho*: Lope in the Tradition of Bawdy," *Bulletin of the Comediantes* 32 (1980), pp. 3-9.

⁴⁰ Victor O. Freeburg, *Disguise Plots in Elizabethan Drama* (New York: Columbia University Press, 1915; reprint Benjamin Blom, 1965), pp. 5-6.

⁴¹ Lope de Vega, *La Dorotea*, I:5; ed. Edwin S. Morby, 2d ed. (Berkeley: University of California Press, 1968), p. 95.

⁴² *La Dorotea* I:1, p. 72; II:2, p. 140.

⁴³ McKendrick, "Women Against Wedlock," p. 116.

⁴⁴ Cervantes provides some notable exceptions. See for example his portrait of Rodolfo

in *La fuerza de la sangre* or of Don Fernando in volume I of *Don Quijote*.

[45] McKendrick, *Woman and Society*, p. 263.

[46] McKendrick, *Woman and Society*, p. 24.

[47] Pike, p. 210.

[48] Perry points out that the so-called "lost women" played an important social and economic function. "Prostitution was commercially profitable for city officials and churchmen as well as street people. It reinforced the authority of the ruling class over unmarried women, folk practitioners, sailors, youths, and quick-fisted dandies. Prostitution was even a form of public assistance, providing jobs for women who would otherwise starve. It strengthened the moral attitudes that supported the city's hierarchy of authority to define and confine evil. Under the guise of public health and public order, it extended the powers of city government. If prostitution was a symptom of social disease, it was also an example of social adaptation. In Seville prostitution helped to preserve the existing social order. It became a useful, practical political tool" (pp. 233-4).

[49] Many "professional" women appear in Lope's theater. See for example *La discreta enamorada*, or *El galán Castrucho* or *El Arenal de Sevilla*.

[50] Angela J. C. Ingram, *In the Posture of a Whore: Changing Attitudes to "Bad" Women in Elizabethan and Jacobean Drama* (Salzburg: Institut für Anglistik und Amerikanistik, 1984), Vol. I.

[51] *Busconas*, too, abound in Golden Age literature. See Cervantes' *El casamiento engañoso [The Bogus Marriage]*, Francisco López de Ubeda's *La pícara Justina*, or Alonso de Castillo Solórzano's *La niña de los embustes*. An early nineteenth-century adaptation of *Fenisa's Hook* is even retitled *La buscona*. See note 1.

[52] McKendrick, *Woman and Society*, p. 316.

[53] Paula S. Berggren, "The Woman's Part: Female Sexuality as Power in Shakespeare's Plays," in Carolyn Ruth Swift Lenz, Gayle Greene and Carol Thomas Neely, *The Woman's Part: Feminist Criticism of Shakespeare* (Urbana: University of Illinois Press, 1980), p. 19.

[54] Ingram, p. 43.

[55] Since Spanish sonnets never ended with a rhyming couplet, as did their Elizabethan counterpart, they avoided the British tendency to round off with a sententious finish. It is conventional to use capital letters to represent the rhyme schemes of long verses such as hendecasyllables and small letters for the rhyme schemes of short verses such as octosyllables.

[56] Verses 950-1 and 1242.

[57] Juan-Germán Schroeder, in his adaptation of this play in 1961, said that he felt compelled to add several verses to clarify that "cat" was a seventeenth-century slang term for "purse," p. 122. Cristóbal de Castro, in his 1912 version, ingenuously suggests that the purse is made of cat skin ("una bolsa de piel de gato"), p. 47. [See note 1.]

El anzuelo de Fenisa

Personas

Camilo	Dinarda	Orozco
Albano	Bernardo	Don Féliz
Fenisa	Fabio	Donato
Celia	Osorio – capitán	Liseo
Lucindo	Campuzano	Estacio
Tristán	Triviño	Un escudero
Dos soldados		

Characters

Camilo	Dinarda	Orozco
Albano	Bernardo	Don Felix
Fenisa	Fabio	Donato
Celia	Captain Osorio	Liseo
Lucindo	Campuzano	Estacio
Tristan	Triviño	A Squire
Two Soldiers		

Jornada Primera

Camilo y Albano

CAMILO: "Que estoy celoso, y voy leyendo en ellas,"
acaba aquel soneto castellano.

ALBANO: ¿Dónde vais a matarme, plantas bellas?

CAMILO: ¿En la arena del mar miras, Albano,
las estampas que deja tu Fenisa?   5

ALBANO: Por ellas sigo su desdén en vano,
    por besar el arena donde pisa.
Temo que el mar deshaga las señales,
excediendo sus márgenes aprisa.

CAMILO: ¿Letras escribe con los pies?

ALBANO: Y tales   10
que leyendo la historia de mis celos,
aprendo penas a la causa iguales.
    No han hecho furia ni rigor los cielos,
para castigo de la humana vida,
que sufran compararse a sus desvelos.   15

CAMILO: Que tenga celos y que celos pida
un hombre que se emplea en gran sujeto,
disculpa me parece conocida;
    porque quien ama, teme; y en efeto,
el temor de quien ama es una cosa   20
que engendra en lo más firme mal conceto;
    pero querer una mujer famosa
en engañar y en no querer ninguno,
supuesto que confieso que es hermosa,
    no tiene igual con desatino alguno;   25
que no llaman celos las traiciones.
Uno ha de amar, y tener celos de uno;
    mas, ¡dónde una mujer forma escuadrones
de tantos hombres, que con menos gente
Alejandro venció dos mil naciones!   30
    Donde hay un galán dentro y otro enfrente,
doce de a pie, cuarenta de a caballo,
tal en la posesión, tal pretendiente,
    vergüenza es ésta, y más que no lo hallo
aun en los animales, pues sabemos   35
que viven cien gallinas con un gallo;
    que glorioso levanta los extremos,
el pardo gamo entre cincuenta gamas,
de las puntas que nunca ofender vemos.

Act I

[The Port of Palermo]
Camilo and Albano

CAMILO: "My jealousy grows great in all I read."*
So ends the sonnet that we learned in Spain.

ALBANO: Oh, footprints, to my death I fear you lead.

CAMILO: Albano, you think footprints will remain
where your Fenisa walked along the sand?   5

ALBANO: They're signs of her contempt; and yet in vain
I look to kiss the place she used to stand.
I fear the sea will wipe the marks away
as it rises and washes clean the strand.

CAMILO: She writes you letters with her feet?

ALBANO: I'll say   10
she does, and every sandy word she writes
gives me good cause for my jealous dismay.
The Heavens, with great noise and fiery lights
have never castigated anyone
the way she's wrecked the slumber of my nights.   15

CAMILO: That doubt and jealousy should overrun
a man whose love is worthy seems to me
exactly right; that's true for everyone;
because all lovers fear; accordingly
these fears engender cruel consternation   20
in men of wisdom and stability.
But to love someone with a reputation
for deceiving, and never loving any,
although her beauty causes admiration,
is an emotion that's not worth a penny.   25
You can't be jealous of such broad deceit:
you get jealous of one rival, not many!
Not of a woman who takes on a fleet.
Why, Alexander, with far fewer men
led twice a thousand nations to defeat!   30
But she has one man in the house, one man
outside, twelve footmen, forty more on horse,
one in her bed, the next in the divan!
It's infamy; this I cannot endorse!
Even the animals don't live like this.   35
We know a hundred chickens run the course
with one single rooster, who struts in bliss;
one handsome buck can do for fifty does
and wear his antlers without prejudice.

---

*This is the closing verse of one of Lope's own sonnets to Micaela Luján. For an analysis of its biographical significance in relation to this play, see D'Antuono, p. 111, n. 16.

	Albano, deste género de damas	40
	huye la bolsa, pon en salvo el oro;	
	que es lo demás andarte por las ramas.	

ALBANO: ¡Qué manso que parece siempre el toro
al que está en la ventana! y al letrado,
¡qué cobarde el flamenco y tibio el moro!   45
    El escribir un libro concertado,
¡qué fácil le parece al ignorante,
y el llevar una cátedra al soldado!
    ¡Qué fácil le parece al estudiante
el conducir la nave al Occidente,   50
la religión al mercader tratante!
    ¡Qué fácil el hablar un presidente,
un rey, un duque a un labrador grosero,
y el olvidar a quien de amor no siente!
    Amor no es calidad, gusto ni fuero;   55
amor no es honra ni es mercadería;
amor no es regidor ni caballero;
    amor es consonancia y armonía
que hacen el deseo y la hermosura,
con que se aumenta cuanto el cielo cría.   60
    Si yo quisiera un bronce, una pintura,
un ave, un árbol, cosa diferente
de mi naturaleza, era locura;
    pero ¿que amar una mujer intente,
juzgas a desatino?

CAMILO: ¡Qué respuesta   65
tan hija de tu amor impertinente!

ALBANO: Mas ¿qué me dices tú que fuera honesta,
dándome con Platón, cuyo aforismo
ya me fastidia y con razón molesta?
    Los que, siendo de amor único abismo   70
dicen que se ha de amar el alma sola,
y que es amor pagalle con el mismo,
    un casto fuego dicen que acrisola
sus sentidos amando, y en secreto
hacen su media noche a la española.   75
    Nerón no confesaba hombre perfeto;
pero decía que en gozar su gusto,
cuál era descompuesto y cuál discreto.
    Si amor es gusto, el que yo tengo es justo.
Ama tú por allá dificultades;   80
que no quiero su bien por su disgusto.

CAMILO: Las virtudes, Albano, y calidades
de una mujer son justo fundamento
de amor, que no las locas liviandades.
    No hay en toda Sicilia (estáme atento),   85
cuanto más en Palermo, donde estamos,

        Albano, stay away from dames like those.   40
    Protect your gold, make sure your purse stays full;
    if not, believe me, you will count your woes.

ALBANO: How utterly innocuous the bull
    seems from the upstairs window; to the clerk
    how tame the Hun, the Moor how affable.   45
        To write a literary masterwork,
    to lecture in a university,
    seem simple to a soldier with his dirk.
        To navigate the reaches of the sea
    is easy for the student anchoret.   50
    The merchant thinks religious life is free.
        How simple for a king, a baronet,
    a duke to talk down to a common man.
    If you've not loved, love's easy to forget!
        Love's not a quality, a whim or plan;   55
    love is not honor, love's not merchandise;
    love's not a ruler, or a gentleman.
        Love is consonance, harmony, a splice
    effected between beauty and desire:
    Heaven made love propagation's device.   60
        If I should love a statue, or aspire
    to a painting, or a tree, or a bird,
    something unnatural, you would inquire
        if I was sane. Yet you say it's absurd
    that I love a woman?

CAMILO: You certify   65
    your lover's foolishness with every word!

ALBANO: Well, how do you expect me to reply,
    beating me on the head with Plato, whose
    tired aphorisms make me want to cry?
        Those whom the utter depths of love excuse   70
    say that the only love's the love of soul,
    that love's return suffices to amuse
        a person, that their hearts are in control,
    burning with a chaste fire; then secretly
    they spend their midnights "a lo español."   75
        Nero, no good himself, said you can see
    in the way humankind partakes of pleasure
    just who is prudent, who's an s. o. b.
        If love is pleasure, mine is cut to measure.
    Go complicate your life; leave me to mine.   80
    Don't give me glum advice and call it treasure.

CAMILO: A woman's virtue is what makes her shine,
    Albano, her good qualities are what
    make her worthy of love, not asinine
        loose living. Not just in Palermo, but   85
    in all of Sicily, now hear me well,

	mujer de más humilde pensamiento.	
	Al puerto, a la ciudad, al monte vamos; allí hallaremos quien sus tretas diga, más que arenas el mar y el bosque ramos.	90
ALBANO:	Lo mismo que te cansa a mí me obliga. Aquella libertad me rinde y mata, y el ver que deje amor e interés siga.	
	Una mujer que quiere y se recata de ofender el galán con pensamientos, aunque la den un Potosí de plata,	95
	allá puede tratar de casamientos; que amor ha de ser fina picardía, poca seguridad, menos contentos.	
	No ha de estar el amor sin compañía, digo sin competencia y sin disgustos; que por la noche es tan hermoso el día.	100
CAMILO:	A fe que habéis hallado vuestro gusto. Si eso es amor, Fenisa es alto objeto. Digo que améis, y que el amarla es justo.	105
ALBANO:	Esotro es amor bobo, éste discreto.	

Fenisa y Celia, con mantos

CELIA:	Admirada, y con razón, Fenisa, de tu venida, muestro tanta confusión.	
FENISA:	Sospecho que se te olvida, Celia...	110
CELIA:	¿Qué?	
FENISA:	Mi condición.	
CELIA:	No sé qué tenga que ver con venir a la Aduana, no siendo tú mercader; pues no eres tú muy liviana, aunque eres libre mujer.	115
FENISA:	Eso te ha de dar aviso de que sin causa no vengo.	
CELIA:	¿Es amor?	
FENISA:	¡Tan de improviso! Pero yo, ¿cuándo le tengo si me adorase Narciso?	120
	Desde el primero que amé, y que a olvidar me enseñó, tan diestra en no amar quedé, que de uno que me burló, en los demás me vengué.	125

	there's no one who's considered more a slut.	
	Ask in town, ask around the docks, and they'll count her tricky schemes for you: more than trees in the forest, beyond what tongues can tell.	90
ALBANO:	These things you censure make me love her; these make me her prisoner; that and the way she gives up love for money with such ease.	
	A woman in love who will not betray her man from fear of giving him a cause to doubt her, though they give her an array of gold — let her get married with her flaws! Love, my friend, is fine mischief; that and greed; it's instability without a pause.	95
	You know love is always accompanied: by rivals, I mean, and by lovers' fights. For late at night the day seems fine indeed.	100
CAMILO:	You've found exactly what you call delight. If that is love, Fenisa can't be beat. Go on, love her, she seems precisely right.	105
ALBANO:	Your kind is stupid love; my kind's discreet.	

Fenisa and Celia, with shawls

CELIA:	I find myself rightly amazed, Fenisa, that you have come here. That is why I appear so dazed.	
FENISA:	Then you have forgotten, I fear, Celia...	110
CELIA:	What?	
FENISA:	...that these are my ways.	
CELIA:	I don't know what your ways have to do with coming down to the port. You're not one of the merchant crew, and you're not one of that loose sort of girl; though you are free, it's true.	115
FENISA:	Well, then, you can be certain this is all planned; I've good reason to come.	
CELIA:	Is it love?	
FENISA:	Sudden thirst for kisses? Not likely! I would not succumb if I were loved by fair Narcissus. Ever since the first man that I loved taught me the way to forget, in not loving I've become spry. One man got to me, and I get revenge on all men in reply.	120 125

       Notablemente se arroja
una mujer a querer,
cuando un gusto se le antoja;
pero más a aborrecer 130
cuando se cansa y se enoja.
       Según corre entre los hombres
esto de amar con engaño,
de mi desdén no te asombres:
basta al cuerdo un desengaño. 135
¿Qué es amor? No me lo nombres.
       No porque yo no perciba
sus regalos y su bien;
pero no es razón que viva
quien nació libre también, 140
de un hombre libre cautiva.
       Yo he dado en esta flaqueza
de burlar cuantos engaña
esto que llaman belleza.

CAMILO:
[aparte a Albano] Celia sola la acompaña. 145

ALBANO: ¿Celia?

CAMILO: No más.

ALBANO: ¡Linda pieza!
¡Extraña imaginación
es venir a la Aduana
deste puerto!

CAMILO: Cosas son
de su condición liviana. 150

ALBANO: Conozco su condición.
       Palermo es famoso puerto
del extranjero, y de trato.
Algún lance ha descubierto.

CAMILO: Ella es de Circe un retrato. 155
De que te ha visto, te advierto.

ALBANO: Hablalla será mejor.
[a Fenisa] ¿Dónde bueno?

FENISA: A ver el mar;
que me agrada su furor.

ALBANO: Todo te suele agradar 160
cuanto carece de amor.
       Este desdén de las ondas,
esta perpetua contienda
te agrada.... Mas no respondas;
por lo que tiene de hacienda, 165

	A woman throws herself with ease	
	into love when she finds someone	
	who knows exactly how to please	
	her. Love may be simply begun,	130
	but when it's over, scorn's a breeze!	
	Since the common practice of men	
	is to love you with false deceit,	
	my scorn should not surprise you, then.	
	You'll fool me once, but not repeat.	135
	Love? I'll not hear the word again.	
	I understand full well when they've	
	shown me the finer points of love.	
	But I was born free, and I'll save	
	my freedom; by the Lord above,	140
	I'll never live as one man's slave!	
	That's why I've chosen as my duty	
	to deceive all who are deceived	
	by this quality they call beauty.	

CAMILO:
[Aside to Albano]   Just Celia's with her, I believe.   145

ALBANO: Celia alone?

CAMILO: Yes.

ALBANO: She's a cutie.
  What an idea, to come call
here at Palermo's Customs Shed.
How odd!

CAMILO: Odd? It's not odd at all,
given the sort of life she's led.   150

ALBANO: I know her well, you will recall.
  Palermo's justly famous port
is where businessmen meet the sea.
She's here for money or for sport.

CAMILO: She's Circe herself: can't you see?   155
She's seen you now, I must report.

ALBANO:
[to Fenisa]   In that case I should speak to her.
Where to?

FENISA: To see the sea. You know
how I like its wild character.

ALBANO: You like everything if there's no   160
trace of love in it I aver.
  The waves' disdain's what you adore;
the crash of surf against the sand
is what you like. Say nothing more.
It's for all the rich goods that land   165

        pienso que su margen rondas.
          ¿En qué rico forastero,
en qué mercader famoso,
en qué extraño marinero,
echas el anzuelo hermoso   170
para buscar su dinero?
          ¿Qué es lo que buscas aquí,
en el puerto deste mar?

FENISA: Seguro estarás de mí
que no te vengo a buscar.   175

ALBANO: Yo vengo a buscarte a ti.

FENISA: ¿Qué me quieres?

ALBANO: Sólo verte,
para alivio de una vida
que has condenado a la muerte.

FENISA: ¿Llamarásme tú homicida?   180

ALBANO: No es poco bien conocerte.

FENISA: Albano, si no has sabido
esta condición que el cielo
me ha dado, que oigas te pido,
porque cese tu desvelo   185
de competir con mi olvido.
      Yo tuve en mi nacimiento
una estrella, que me obliga
a que en este mar violento
peces busque, peces siga   190
como otros, aves del viento.
      ¿No has visto que un gran señor
va por los valles y cerros,
despeñado cazador,
ya con aves, ya con perros,   195
sin temer nieve o calor?
      Pues eso mesmo hay en mí;
pero apliquéme a pescar,
y a eso vengo por aquí;
tiendo la red en el mar,   200
que es la estrella en que nací.
      Ojos y lengua son cebo
del anzuelo deste amor;
si pica y es bobo y nuevo,
doyle cuerda, y del favor   205
asido un año le llevo.
      Si es ladino y está diestro,
aunque caiga, vuelve al mar,
porque ofendida me muestro

	here, that's what makes you like the shore.	
	What rich stranger do you coerce?	
	What foreign sailors draw your look?	
	With what rich businessman converse?	
	Where will you sink your lovely hook	170
	to fish out a fat bulging purse?	
	What have your eyes lit on today	
	here on the shoreline of the sea?	
FENISA:	You should have no fear that I'll say	
	that you are what I've come to see.	175
ALBANO:	I'm looking for you anyway.	
FENISA:	What do you want?	
ALBANO:	To look at you:	
	one single look will surely save	
	the life of one you coldly slew.	
FENISA:	You think I've put you in your grave?	180
ALBANO:	Just knowing you sufficed to do it.	
FENISA:	Albano, aren't you aware	
	of this condition that the Fates	
	have given me? If not, prepare	
	to listen 'til your grief abates;	185
	stop struggling with my lack of care.	
	There was a star the day that I	
	was born, a planet that inclined	
	me to the sea, and there to try	
	to look for fish, to fishes find,	190
	as others seek birds in the sky.	
	Have you not seen how a great lord	
	crosses valleys, climbs mountain sides,	
	hunting together with his horde,	
	the swooping hawk, the hound that strides,	195
	through snow and heat, all one accord?	
	I am driven by the same drive,	
	but the shore is my hunting ground;	
	that's why I came down here, to strive	
	with my nets in the salty sound;	200
	that's how my star keeps me alive.	
	On this sweet lover's hook of mine	
	the bait I use are eyes and tongue.	
	Whoever nibbles at my twine,	
	if he's foolish enough, and young,	205
	one year I play him on my line.	
	But if he's clever, though he took	
	the bait I let him slip away.	
	I won't give him another look	

       que, si no ha de aprovechar, 210
ocupe el anzuelo nuestro.
    Si yo viese la hermosura
mayor que naturaleza
ha dado a mortal criatura;
si viese más gentileza, 215
más tierno amor, más blandura;
    si viese por mí llorar;
si me viese eternizar
más que Laura y que Beatriz;
si viese un mozo infeliz 220
de mis balcones colgar;
    si viese que por Fenisa
Píramo se pasa el pecho,
y a Leandro ya en camisa,
mientras no viese provecho, 225
todo era cosa de risa.

CAMILO: ¿Oístelo?

ALBANO: Ya lo oí.
Escucha, Fenisa.

FENISA: Di.

ALBANO: Si hubiese quien te llorase,
te amase... y te regalase... 230
¿Tendríasle amor?

FENISA: Eso sí.

ALBANO: ¿Con qué te contentarás
para prueba deste amor?

FENISA: Necio por extremo estás.
¿Quiéresme entender mejor? 235

ALBANO: Sí.

FENISA: Pues declárome más.
   Quien tiene un jardín, ¿qué hace?
Riega, regala, cultiva
la yerba o árbol que nace,
para que después reciba 240
el fruto que satisface.
   Quien tiene un caballo hermoso,
asiste a verle comer,
de su estancia cuidadoso;
hasta el herrar quiere ver, 245
de sus estampas curioso.
   Mira el freno y el bocado
que lengua y boca no ofenda,
Tráele bien enjaezado,

	if there's no profit; there's no way	210
	I'll keep him dangling on my hook.	
	If I should see the loveliest	
	form that Dame Nature ever filled,	
	that ever mortal creature blessed;	
	if I should see a love more skilled,	215
	more gentle than the gentlest;	
	if I were to see someone weep	
	for me, write me more poetry	
	than even Beatrice did reap;	
	or Laura; if some youth I'd see	220
	from my window attempt to leap;	
	if Piramus on my behalf	
	were to stab himself one sad minute;	
	if Leander should appear half	
	dressed, and there was no profit in it—	225
	why, all of it would make me laugh!	
CAMILO:	Did you hear that?	
ALBANO:	I understood	
	it all. Fenisa...	
FENISA:	Well, what is it?	
ALBANO:	If someone should weep for you, should	
	love you, and when he comes to visit	230
	should bring gifts, you'd love him?	
FENISA:	I would.	
ALBANO:	Then what would it take to convince	
	you his devotion was sincere?	
FENISA:	You're such a ninny. I won't mince	
	words with you. Do you want to hear	235
	my meaning?	
ALBANO:	Yes.	
FENISA:	Here are some hints.	
	What then does a gardener do?	
	He waters, feeds, and cultivates	
	the shoot or seedling when it's new;	
	he tends it carefully and waits	240
	to reap all the fruits that ensue.	
	One who owns a thoroughbred horse	
	goes to the barn to watch him eat.	
	He cleans out the stable, of course.	
	He'll even watch the blacksmith heat	245
	the iron, he judges the force	
	with which he taps the shoes. He tries	
	the reins himself, he checks the bit,	
	he adjusts the harness to size	

	y por puntos le encomienda	250
	al solícito criado.	
	Bozales le manda hacer,	
	y rizar y componer	
	de bandas de bizarría;	
	y todo esto para un día	255
	en que le quiere correr.	
	¿Hasme entendido?	
Albano:	Bien creo	
	que te entiendo.	
Fenisa:	Pues ¿qué aguardas	
	a conocer mi deseo?	

[Hablan bajo Albano y Fenisa.]
Lucindo y Tristán

Lucindo:		
[a Tristán]	¿Has contentado las guardas?	260
Tristán:	Que quedan contentas creo.	
	Toda la ropa está fuera,	
	No queda cosa en la nave.	
Lucindo:	¡Oh, Sicilia!	
Tristán:	¿Qué te altera?	
Lucindo:	¡Qué bien, tras tanto mar, sabe,	265
	Tristán, la verde ribera!	
Tristán:	Diráslo por las mujeres	
	que pasean por la playa.	
Lucindo:	¡Qué mal conocerme quieres!	
	No hayas miedo tú que vaya	270
	por el mar de sus placeres	
	esta nave de mi edad,	
	aunque bonanza prometa;	
	porque no hay seguridad	
	en la mujer más perfeta,	275
	de mudanza o libertad.	
	Advierte que no te digo	
	perfecta en virtud.	
Tristán:	Pues, ¿qué?	
Lucindo:	En amar.	
Tristán:	A amor bendigo.	
	¡Plega a Dios que no te dé	280
	de esa libertad castigo!	
Lucindo:	Si mi padre aquí me envía	
	desde Valencia, Tristán,	
	con esta mercadería,	

	and he makes certain to outfit	250
	his groom with the finest supplies.	
	He puts medallions on the reins	
	and weaves ribbons into its tail;	
	its mane he drapes with silken skeins.	
	And all of this to what avail?	255
	To race one day for all those pains!	
	Have you got it now?	

ALBANO: Your design
is quite clear.

FENISA: Well then, why are you
waiting there if you know my mind?

[Albano and Fenisa speak quietly.]
Lucindo, Tristan [and the above]

LUCINDO:
[to Tristan]   Have you given the guards their due?   260

TRISTAN: I have. They're quite content you'll find.
      The sails are stowed, the bags in hand,
there is nothing left on the boat.

LUCINDO: Oh, Sicily!

TRISTAN: Why, what's so grand?

LUCINDO: After so many months afloat   265
how fine it is to tread dry land!

TRISTAN: Don't tell me you're not looking for
the girls who on this beach parade?

LUCINDO: You must not know me anymore!
There's no reason to be afraid   270
my tender young ship will explore
   these seas of pleasure, though I see
good sailing everywhere. I've come
to think there's no security,
in the most perfect woman, from   275
wild freedom or inconstancy.
   And notice that I do not say
perfect in virtue.

TRISTAN: Speak your mind.

LUCINDO: I mean perfect in love.

TRISTAN: Hooray
for that sort! Still, I hope their kind   280
of freedom won't lead you astray.

LUCINDO: But, Tristan, if my father sent
me here from Valencia to sell
in Palermo his whole shipment;

y mis deudos, que allá están, 285
con hacienda suya o mía;
  si de lo que he de vender
tengo de cargar de trigo,
¿por qué me nombras mujer,
que es el mayor enemigo 290
del trato del mercader?
  Ni el fiar ni el porfiar,
ni el alzarse, ni el quebrar,
ni el no pagar los señores,
ni el morirse los deudores, 295
ni la inclemencia del mar,
  igualan a que se arroje
un mercader a querer,
ni hay pirata que despoje
como una hermosa mujer 300
que entre los brazos le coge.

TRISTÁN: ¡Plega al cielo que te dure
tan alto conocimiento!

ALBANO:
[a Fenisa]   En fin, ¿dices que procure
regalarte?

FENISA: Ese es mi intento, 305
porque el amor se asegure;
  que no puede amor durar
sin fundamento y estribo.

ALBANO: Y ¿qué es el estribo?

FENISA: El dar,
porque es, no habiendo dativo, 310
cantar mal y porfiar.

ALBANO: Voy a tratar de tu gusto;
dame esta noche licencia.

FENISA: Si me regalas, ¿no es justo?

[Vase retirando Albano.]

ALBANO:
[a Camilo] Perdiendo voy la paciencia. 315

CAMILO: Yo siento vuestro disgusto.
  ¿Pensáis regalarla?

ALBANO: Sí;
que estoy muriendo por ella.

CAMILO: ¿No os desapasiona aquí
verla interesable?

	and if our investors, as well,	285
	entrusted me their consignment;	
	and if after with what I'm paid	
	I'm supposed to load up with wheat,	
	don't talk women to me! A maid	
	leads any merchant to defeat.	290
	They're the worst enemy of trade.	
	Neither debt nor insolvency,	
	nor broken trust nor broken wills,	
	neither bad credit nor bankruptcy,	
	nor debtor's death with unpaid bills,	295
	not even wild tempests at sea	
	are a fraction as bad as when	
	a merchant throws himself at love!	
	No pirate ever despoiled men	
	like a clinging woman whose glove	300
	gets into their pockets.	

TRISTAN: Amen!
                      I hope to Heaven this good sense
                      endures until the end of time.

ALBANO:
[to Fenisa]   You mean I'm to spare no expense
                      in courting you?

FENISA: Yes, that's what I'm   305
                      saying, unless you would dispense
                          with my love. Love will not endure
                      unless it has good buttressing.

ALBANO: What's buttressing?

FENISA: Divestiture.
                      Unless you let your money sing,   310
                      I'll find sour any overture.

ALBANO: I'll try it your way for a change.
                      Give me leave to see you tonight.

FENISA: If you'll *pay* court, then it's arranged.

[Albano makes to leave.]

ALBANO:
[to Camilo]   All my patience has taken flight.   315

CAMILO: I don't find your reaction strange.
                        Will you give her something?

ALBANO: I guess
                      I will, since I'm dying for her.

CAMILO: Doesn't it make you love her less
                      that she's so greedy?

ALBANO: Es bella,   320
             y más me amartela ansí;
             este interés y desdén
             me obliga a ver si la venzo.

[Vanse Albano y Camilo.]

FENISA:
[aparte a Celia]   El hombre parece bien.

CELIA: Pues llega a hablarle.

FENISA: Comienzo.   325
             ¿Fuéronse?

CELIA: Ya no se ven.

FENISA: ¿Parécete pez el hombre
             que me será de provecho?

CELIA: Llega, y pregunta su nombre.

FENISA: ¡Por mi vida, que es bien hecho!   330
[a Lucindo] Dios os guarde, gentilhombre.

LUCINDO: Y a vos os dé un rico esposo,
             si sois libre; y si tenéis
             marido, pues fue dichoso
             en ser vuestro, le gocéis   335
             sin pensamiento celoso.
                  ¿Qué es lo que queréis de mí?

FENISA: ¿Cuándo llegastes aquí?

LUCINDO: Hoy vi la tierra y la aurora
             juntas, pero el sol agora;   340
             que hasta veros no le vi.

FENISA: Con poética licencia
             me habéis hecho vuestro sol.

LUCINDO: Diómela vuestra presencia.

FENISA: ¿Qué nación?

LUCINDO: Soy español.   345

FENISA: ¿De qué parte?

LUCINDO: De Valencia.

FENISA: Si fuérades de Toledo,
             tenía qué preguntaros.

LUCINDO: Sólo de Valencia puedo...

[Hablan bajo Lucindo y Fenisa.]

TRISTÁN:
[a Celia]   ¿Puedo yo también hablaros?   350

ALBANO: Her allure 320
is beauty. I'm stuck, I confess.
Her greed and her disdain entice
me most her affection to win.

[Camilo and Albano exit.]

FENISA:
[to Celia] That young man over there seems nice.

CELIA: Why don't you go and talk to him? 325

FENISA: And the others?

CELIA: Run off like mice.

FENISA: Now there's a handsome visitor!
Think he's a good fish for my hook?

CELIA: Go ask the name of this señor.

FENISA: You know, I think I like his look. 330
[to Lucindo] Hello. God keep you, gentle sir.

LUCINDO: May he grant you a good husband
if you're single; and if you be
married, as your husband has grand
fortune in you, may jealousy 335
from your life be forever banned.
Tell me what I can do for you.

FENISA: Tell me, when did your ship touch shore?

LUCINDO: I just saw land and the dawn too.
But I'd not seen the sun before 340
until you came into my view.

FENISA: With the license of poetry
you have rechristened me your sun.

LUCINDO: Your presence brought the sun to me.

FENISA: What land is yours?

LUCINDO: From Spain I've come. 345

FENISA: What part?

LUCINDO: Valencia, by the sea.

FENISA: If Toledo were home I'd fill
up your ears with my questioning.

LUCINDO: If you want Valencia, I will...

[Lucindo and Fenisa speak quietly.]

TRISTAN:
[to Celia] How about I ask you something? 350

CELIA:	Bien puede, estándose quedo.	
TRISTÁN:	Va de quedo, y digo ansí:	
	¿Quién es aquesta su ama?	
CELIA:	Una dama.	
TRISTÁN:	¿Dama?	
CELIA:	Sí.	
TRISTÁN:	Y ¿de qué manera es dama?	355
CELIA:	¿Eso me pregunta a mí?	
TRISTÁN:	Pues ¿está mal preguntado?	
CELIA:	¿Cómo es el hombre?	

TRISTÁN:	Formado	
	de cuatro elementos soy,	
	tengo alma y cuerpo, y estoy	360
	de potencias adornado;	
	diferénciome a mujer	
	en las barbas y el valor.	
	No me mande proceder,	
	sino advierta que en rigor	365
	dama es oficio, y no es ser.	
	Doncellas suelen decir	
	muchas, sin advertir	
	que se han de diferenciar;	
	que hay doncellas de casar,	370
	y doncellas de servir;	
	y así, dama ha de tener	
	su diferencia forzosa.	
CELIA:	Por lo menos es mujer	
	discreta, gallarda, hermosa,	375
	y de honrado proceder.	

TRISTÁN:	Y ¿qué busca por aquí?	
CELIA:	Nuevas de un perdido hermano.	
TRISTÁN:	Peligro correis ansí.	
CELIA:	¿Peligro?	
TRISTÁN:	Luego ¿no es llano?	380
CELIA:	¿No es tierra segura?	
TRISTÁN:	Sí;	
	pero el mar, que estos altivos	
	peñascos quiere exceder	
	y sus límites nativos,	

CELIA:	You can if you keep your hands still.	
TRISTAN:	One thing — and I won't touch your dress — who's that mistress of yours I see?	
CELIA:	A lady.	
TRISTAN:	Just a lady?	
CELIA:	Yes.	
TRISTAN:	Just what kind of lady is she?	355
CELIA:	Your question causes me distress.	
TRISTAN:	What's wrong with my question?	
CELIA:	What kind of man are you then?	
TRISTAN:	I am made of four elements; I've a mind, a soul, and a body; arrayed with a few powers; but you'll find two things, under close observation, that I've got and girls haven't got: courage and beard. This explanation is done. Besides, "lady" is not a title, it's an occupation. Call someone a "maid," but observe that two meanings are merited: there are distinctions to preserve. Some "maids" are ready to be wed; and some "maids" are suited to serve. So there must be some difference among kinds of ladies.	360 365 370
CELIA:	Let me describe to you her excellence: she's lovely, smart, and totally of honorable innocence.	375
TRISTAN:	What is she looking for down here?	
CELIA:	News of a lost brother of hers.	
TRISTAN:	Then that you're in danger is clear.	
CELIA:	Danger?	
TRISTAN:	Yes; maybe even worse.	380
CELIA:	This land's not safe?	
TRISTAN:	Yes, but I fear that the ocean, belligerent to a fault, which strives to attack the shore, to extend the extent	

	sin duda os quiere prender	385
	por pescados fugitivos.	
CELIA:	¡Lindo bellaco!	
TRISTÁN:	¿Yo lindo?	
CELIA:	¿Tú conmigo españolizas?	
FENISA: *[a Lucindo]*	Digo, mi bien, que me rindo.	
LUCINDO:	Esta humildad solemnizas.	390
FENISA:	Dime tu nombre.	
LUCINDO:	Lucindo.	
FENISA:	Si nombre de luz tenías,	
	¿qué mucho que me encendieses?	
LUCINDO:	Las desconfianzas mías	
	querría que conocieses.	395
FENISA:	Español, ¿tú desconfías?	
LUCINDO:	Pues, ¿no ha de desconfiar	
	un forastero?	
FENISA:	No sé...	
	¡Nunca yo viniera al mar,	
	pues otro en su playa hallé,	400
	donde me pienso anegar!	
LUCINDO:	¿Que te he parecido bien?	
FENISA:	No sé cómo te encarezcan	
	estos mis ojos tan bien	
	ese talle, sin que crezcan	405
	las aguas del mar que ven.	
	Pero, ¿qué digo? No más.	
	Loca estoy. Hombre, ¿qué es esto?	
	¡Jesús! ¿Qué hechizos me das?	
LUCINDO:	¡Tan presto!	
FENISA:	¡Ay, Dios! Véte presto:	410
	mas, espera; ¿adónde vas?	
LUCINDO:	A la posada; es forzoso.	

	of its domain, will take you back like fish out of your element.	385
CELIA:	What a sweet rogue!	
TRISTAN:	You call me sweet?	
CELIA:	You try your Spanish tricks on me?	
FENISA: [to Lucindo]	My darling, I accept defeat.	
LUCINDO:	I'm moved by your humility.	390
FENISA:	What's your name?	
LUCINDO:	Lucindo.	
FENISA:	You treat me to the light* that's caught in your name. It's no wonder I'm on fire.	
LUCINDO:	I hear you, but I'm still unsure somehow. My principles require me to tell you.	395
FENISA:	So you're not sure, Spaniard?	
LUCINDO:	Don't you think I should be wary? I am a stranger here.	
FENISA:	I wish I'd not come to the sea to drown my sorrows, for I fear I've found another, dear to me.	400
LUCINDO:	Then, Fenisa, you think I'm nice?	
FENISA:	I don't know how I can explain how special you are to these eyes that make the sea swell from my pain and overflow from liquid cries. 　But what am I saying? No more of this! I must have lost my mind! How have you bewitched me?	405
LUCINDO:	Before an hour is past?	
FENISA:	Get thee behind me. Stop! What are you going for?	410
LUCINDO:	To find lodgings. I have to go.	

---

*Lucindo's name suggests the Spanish word for light (*luz*) and for fire (*incendio*).

FENISA:	Si por mis deudos no fuera,	
	dulce español generoso,	
	en mi casa te la diera,	415
	como en el alma es forzoso;	
	pero bien podrás entrar	
	con decir que de mi hermano	
	sabes nuevas.	
LUCINDO:	¿Qué hay lugar?	
FENISA:	Sígueme.	
LUCINDO:	Dame esa mano,	420
	que te la quiero besar.	
FENISA:	Espera; a Celia hablaré,	
	para que avisada esté.	
LUCINDO:	Y yo a este criado mío.	
FENISA:	Celia...	
CELIA:	Señora...	
FENISA: *[aparte a Celia]*	Confío	425
	que lo que buscaba hallé.	
	No ha venido forastero	
	a Sicilia en muchos años,	
	mercadero o caballero,	
	donde puedan mis engaños	430
	pescar tan lindo dinero.	
	Una nave trae cargada	
	de paños, medias y rasos.	
CELIA:	¿Hate dicho la posada?	
FENISA:	Ya la sé.	
CELIA:	¡Dichosos pasos,	435
	y tarde bien empleada!	
	Y ¿qué modo de hombre es él?	
	¿Es novicio moscatel	
	o discreto vergonzoso?	
	¿Procede a lo generoso?	440
FENISA:	Cayó como mosca en miel;	
	díjele cuatro dulzuras,	
	encarecíle su talle,	
	y está mortal.	
CELIA:	¿Qué procuras?	
FENISA:	El cuerpo en cueros dejalle,	445
	y el alma con mataduras;	

FENISA:	If it were not that I have kin, sweet, generous Spaniard, you know that my own house could be your inn, as my soul is your studio. But they will let you in with this stratagem: say you have some news from my brother.	415
LUCINDO:	I am in bliss: you have room?	
FENISA:	Come on. Don't refuse.	420
LUCINDO:	You must give me your hand to kiss.	
FENISA:	Let me talk to Celia before we go about what to expect.	
LUCINDO:	I'll have to tell my man the score.	
FENISA:	Celia.	
CELIA:	My lady.	
FENISA: [aside to Celia]	I suspect I've found what I was looking for. No one has made this big a splash in Sicily for a long time. I've never seen a merchant flash so much money. With my tricks I'm certain to fish up all his cash. His boat is full of excellent cloth and all sorts of finery.	425 430
CELIA:	Do you know to which inn he went?	
FENISA:	I do.	
CELIA:	How lucky can we be! How well this afternoon we've spent. What kind of a man have we got? A bright youngster his first time out or some discreet, shameless old sot? Will he spread his money about?	435 440
FENISA:	A fly in honey's what we've caught. I told him three or four sweet words; I said how goodlooking he was. He's as good as dead!	
CELIA:	What reward's in it?	
FENISA:	I'll leave him naked as a jaybird, his soul slashed by swords.	445

	tápate y vamos de aquí,	
	porque nos venga siguiendo.	

[Vanse las dos.]

Tristán:	¿Eso te ha pasado?	
Lucindo:	Sí.	
Tristán:	¿Qué mujer es?	
Lucindo:	No lo entiendo.	450
Tristán:	Mas ¿que se burla de ti?	
Lucindo:	¡De mí! Pues ¿qué me ha tomado?	
Tristán:	¿Qué piensas tú que es mirar	
	y hablar tierno y regalado?	
	Escrituras de pagar	455
	lo que se hubiere gozado.	
	Y para que no te asombre	
	esta mi nueva opinión,	
	advierte que hablando un hombre	
	con las mujeres que son	460
	deste trato y deste nombre.	
	Los ojos están diciendo:	
	"Sepan cuantos ésta vieren,	
	que nos estamos rindiendo	
	a pagar cuanto quisieren	465
	los que nos están vendiendo.	
	Y renunciamos las leyes	
	que al discreto dan los reyes,	
	y al galán por su decoro;	
	mas no sé si las de Toro;	470
	que donde hay labranza, hay bueyes.	
	Solamente mientras trata,	
	la de la *non numerata*	
	pecunia, queda en su fuerza."	
Lucindo:	Aquí, Tristán, ¿quién me fuerza,	475
	quién me obliga, quién me mata?	
	Si dije que iría tras ella,	
	fue porque la vi tan bella;	
	pero también puede ser	
	una principal mujer	480
	y alguna ilustre doncella.	

	Let's make them follow. Fix your dress; cover yourself, it's time to go.	

[The two exit.]

TRISTAN:	Then that's what happened to you.	
LUCINDO:	Yes.	
TRISTAN:	Who is the woman?	
LUCINDO:	I don't know.	450
TRISTAN:	That she mocks you is what I'd guess.	
LUCINDO:	Mocks me? What has she got with me?	
TRISTAN:	What do you think those sexy looks are for, that sweet gentility? She's writing in her account books how much she'll get as pleasure's fee. Now don't you go into a pique, for what I'm going to say is so: when you see a man cheek to cheek with this kind of woman, you know that whatever his lips may speak, what his eyes tell you is precise: "Know ye, whoever may behold us: we'll make any sacrifice to take whatever goods are sold and pay whatever is the price. And henceforth we renounce the laws that kings have set to keep young men discreet and to give gallants pause." Unless it's Toro's laws again,* what with their bulls and horns. Because unless I'm completely misled, and she keeps the law of *Count Not Your Coins*, you'll lose more than your head.	455 460 465 470
LUCINDO:	Tristan, who forces me? Who's got me on the ropes? Who shoots me dead? If I said to you I would chase after her, it's that I acclaim her beauty. It could be the case that she's a well-born maid, a dame most illustrious in this place.	475 480

---

*The laws proclaimed by Ferdinand and Isabel in the city of Toro in 1504 encouraged the nobility to form great landed estates through marriage. The reference is to the economics of marriage, and since *toro* means bull, also to the horns of cuckoldry and deception.

Tristán:	Doncella e ilustre no; que mujer que tiene lustre, con alguno se le dio.	
Lucindo:	Pues siendo una dama ilustre, ¿qué pierdo en servirla yo?	485
Tristán:	¡Dama ilustre junto al mar!	
Lucindo:	¿No pudo salir a ver?	
Tristán:	Pudo salir a pescar; buscona debe de ser: mas ¿qué te ha de rebuscar?	490
Lucindo:	Ahora bien, ¿qué puede hacer esta mujer, si es mujer que busca?	
Tristán:	Notable daño, porque de su falso engaño todo se puede creer.	495
Lucindo:	¿Es tomarme mi dinero?	
Tristán:	Y eso, ¿es poco?	
Lucindo:	No he vendido, puesto que vender espero lo que a Sicilia he traído.	500
Tristán:	Tú eres lindo majadero. ¿No se lo darás después?	
Lucindo:	No la veré después.	
Tristán:	Vamos; que apenas mueve los pies para que no la perdamos. Pero temo que la des el dinerillo que llevas.	505
Lucindo:	Guarda tú la bolsa allá.	
Tristán:	Muestra; pero no te atrevas a dar la cadena.	
Lucindo:	Está con llave y con guardas nuevas.	510
Tristán:	¡Quítatela, por mi vida!	
Lucindo:	Toma; guárdala también.	
Tristán:	No te enfades que te pida esas dos sortijas.	
Lucindo:	Bien.	515
Tristán:	Es esa piedra escogida;	

TRISTAN:	Not illustrious, and a maid...?	
	A maid with so much lustre must	
	be buffed with something or she'll fade.	
LUCINDO:	She *is* illustrious, I trust.	485
	Why would you have me be afraid?	
TRISTAN:	Illustrious? Here at the port?	
LUCINDO:	Maybe she's just come for a look.	
TRISTAN:	No way! She's the gold digging sort!	
	She's down here with bait on her hook.	490
	But why's she set you up for sport?	
LUCINDO:	Even if all that should be true,	
	what can she do? Even if she's	
	a gold digger?	
TRISTAN:	What can she do?	
	She is as false as she can be.	495
	She can do everything to you!	
LUCINDO:	You think it's my money she's after?	
TRISTAN:	That's not enough?	
LUCINDO:	I've still not sold	
	a thing. My boat's full to the rafters	
	and I've still not seen any gold.	500
TRISTAN:	You dolt, you make me shake with laughter.	
	Later you'll give her everything.	
LUCINDO:	I won't see her later.	
TRISTAN:	Let's go.	
	Look how her feet are dawdling	
	from trying to keep us in tow.	505
	But won't you be surrendering	
	even what cash you've got with you?	
LUCINDO:	Then take my purse into your care.	
TRISTAN:	Give it here. Whatever you do,	
	don't give her your chain.	
LUCINDO:	It's safe where	510
	it is; even the clasp is new.	
TRISTAN:	Take it off, then, for pity's sake.	
LUCINDO:	Alright. Here's something else to hold.	
TRISTAN:	Forgive me, but it's a mistake	
	to wear those two gold rings.	
LUCINDO:	I'm sold.	515
TRISTAN:	That stone's well chosen, not a fake.	

	que el decir que los amantes	
	tiran por las calles piedras,	
	es por piedras semejantes;	
	que una piedra, tales hiedras	520
	son a consumir bastantes.	
LUCINDO:	Eso se suele entender	
	porque locos suelen ser.	
TRISTÁN:	Otro sentido has de dalle.	
	Diamantes echa en la calle	525
	quien sirve una vil mujer.	
LUCINDO:	Sin diamantes ni dinero	
	y sin cadena voy.	
TRISTÁN:	Vamos;	
	que si mar la considero,	
	con causa nos desnudamos	530
	para pasarla primero.	

[Vanse.]
Dinarda, de camino, en hábito de hombre; Bernardo y Fabio

DINARDA:	Parece que escupe el mar	
	muchachos a la ribera.	
BERNARDO:	La tierra sé que me espera,	
	la tierra quiero besar.	535
FABIO:	Es madre la tierra, en fin,	
	y como madre sustenta.	
DINARDA:	¡Qué temeraria tormenta!	
BERNARDO:	No te faltara un delfín,	
	en quien hallaras ventura,	540
	que te sacara del mar,	
	como al otro por cantar,	
	a ti por tanta hermosura.	
DINARDA:	¿Qué habemos de hacer los tres,	
	ya que a Sicilia llegamos,	545
	sin dineros y sin amos?	
BERNARDO:	Servir.	
DINARDA:	¿Servir?	
BERNARDO:	Servir, pues.	
DINARDA:	Yo pienso hacerme soldado,	
	y sueldo de rey tirar.	

	You know the line: "I love you more, love, than there are stones in the street"? No matter what you've heard before, these are the stones that make hearts beat. This ivy ties you to the floor!	520
LUCINDO:	What you say's a common conceit; but as a saying it's insane.	
TRISTAN:	Then here's another to repeat: "Who loves a woman vile and vain is throwing diamonds in the street."	525
LUCINDO:	I've given my money away, my chain and diamonds too.	
TRISTAN:	Let's go. If she's an ocean, then I say to strip yourself is right, you know, since in her waves you'll surely play.	530

[*They exit.*]
Dinarda, in men's travel clothing; Bernardo and Fabio

DINARDA:	So many young men prowl the sand, it seems the ocean spits them up.	
BERNARDO:	Dry land welcomes me now; my cup is full. How fine to kiss the land.	535
FABIO:	Well, the earth's our mother, they say; and like a mother, she provides.	
DINARDA:	What fearful stormy wind and tides!	
BERNARDO:	Then some dolphin will come your way, bring you good luck and do his duty saving you from the ocean's waves; If Arion* for his song he saves, perhaps he'll save you for your beauty.	540
DINARDA:	How shall the three of us live, when we have arrived in this condition: without money, or a position?	545
BERNARDO:	Be servants.	
DINARDA:	Servants?	
BERNARDO:	Servants, then.	
DINARDA:	There's soldiering. Why not repair to the army to earn our living?	

---

*Arion, poet and singer of Methymna in Lesbos, was rescued from drowning by a dolphin. Ovid: *Fasti*, 2:79; Virgil, *Eclogues*, 8:56.

Fabio:	Yo no me pienso soldar,	550
	porque nunca fui quebrado;	
	pero si hay un capitán	
	le llevaré la jineta.	
Bernardo:	¡Por Dios, que es cosa sujeta!	
Fabio:	Cuantos nacieron lo están.	555
Bernardo:	¿Cuantos nacieron?	
Fabio:	Sí.	
Bernardo:	¿Cómo?	
Fabio:	El rey sirve de ser rey,	
	de hacer justicia, dar ley;	
	el señor, de mayordomo,	
	de camarero, de ser	560
	gentilhombre o de la boca,	
	o el oficio que le toca	
	a su pesar o placer;	
	el prelado, de acudir	
	a su iglesia diligente,	565
	al gobierno el presidente,	
	el oidor también a oír.	
	El alguacil a prender;	
	el alcalde a castigar;	
	el que es letrado a abogar,	570
	a defender u ofender;	
	al proceso el escribano,	
	al enfermo el que es doctor,	
	el oficial al señor,	
	y al hidalgo el que es villano;	575
	la casada a su marido,	
	a su padre la doncella,	
	y el padre le sirve a ella	
	en la comida y vestido.	
	Mas ¿de qué sirve alargarse?	580
	¿Quién hay que no sirva aquí	
	en darse a comer a sí,	
	en vestirse y desnudarse?	
	Dïógenes con ventaja	
	solamente no sirvió;	585
	pero dicen que vivió	
	metido en una tinaja.	
Bernardo:	Verdad es que a sí o alguno,	
	todos sirven; mas quisiera	
	que entre los tres no sirviera	590
	ninguno, Fabio, a ninguno.	
	Los tres somos españoles,	
	que en saliendo de su tierra,	

FABIO:	I'm not broken, so don't be giving	550
	my bones for repair. But I swear	
	that what I *will* do, if you find	
	me a captain, is hold his horse.	
BERNARDO:	I think that subject's run its course.	
FABIO:	But subject's how we're all defined.	555
BERNARDO:	Subject?	
FABIO:	Every man alive.	
BERNARDO:	What?	

FABIO: The king is subject to his subjects;
he must rule or everyone objects.
Every great lord is on the spot:
  he must be majordomo or   560
butler, serving at the king's table,
or valet, whatever he's able
to do and the king wants him for.
  The prelate must show he's god-fearing
in church every day without fail.   565
The sheriff must look to his jail;
and the judge has to hear his hearings.
  The president has to preside;
the bailiff's required to arrest;
the lawyer must argue his best,   570
that is, once he's chosen which side.
  The court clerk's obliged to record;
the ailing oblige the physician;
the officer serves the patrician;
the villager's bound to his lord.   575
  The husband is served by his spouse;
the maiden's obliged to her father,
while he's obligated to bother
himself with food, clothing and house.
  So don't get yourself in a heat,   580
for serving is everyone's fate:
we all serve when we salivate,
for service gets us food to eat.
  They say that old Diogenes
is the one man who never served;   585
but he lived the way he deserved:
in a vat, as drunk as you please.

BERNARDO: We all serve. In a general
way everyone's a servant; we
all know that. But I'd like us three,   590
Fabio, to serve no one at all.
  For we three come from Spanish states:
and when we leave our country, for

| | o sea en paz o sea en guerra,
se hace príncipes y soles.
   Hagamos lo mismo acá,
y pues de España venimos,
parezcamos lo que fuimos. | 595 |

DINARDA: Bien dice.

FABIO: Bien dicho está. 600
  Oíd: echemos los tres
suertes quién será el señor,
y al que saliere, en rigor
sirvan los dos.

DINARDA: Justo es.

BERNARDO: Añadirémosle un don,
diremos que es caballero, 605
y aunque con poco dinero,
tendrá mucha presunción.
  Acudirá a los soldados,
acompañará al Virrey,
daréle ventaja el Rey 610
y las pagas de criados,
  con que alguna principal
mujer de Sicilia venga,
donde por ventura tenga
ventura a español igual. 615
  ¿Qué os parece?

DINARDA: Que pareces
hombre de Toledo, en fin.

BERNARDO: ¿No es mejor que un amo ruin?

DINARDA: Digo que sí treinta veces;
  porque, en efecto, es servir 620
a un bellaco mentecato,
que a tres horas tire un plato.

FABIO: Sí; pero habéis de advertir
  que en entrando en la posada,
juntos hemos de comer; 625
porque señor no ha de haber
si está la puerta cerrada.

DINARDA: Bien dicho.

BERNARDO: Pues va de suerte
tres reales que tengo aquí.

FABIO: ¿Son de España todos?

BERNARDO: Sí. 630

	peaceful trade, or for strident war,	
	we shine like suns or potentates.	595
	That's what we should be doing here;	
	and since from Spain we've come this far,	
	let us behave like what we are.	

DINARDA: That's perfect.

FABIO: Yes it is; that's clear.
I know what we'll do: let's all three 600
draw lots to see which will be lord.
The winner will have as reward
two servants.

DINARDA: That's alright with me.

BERNARDO: We'll add a title, call him sir,
say that he's a knight from someplace, 605
with little money to his face
but proud as any emperor.
  He'll go where the best soldiers go;
accompany the viceroy too.
The king himself he will outdo; 610
his servants will put on a show,
  and this behavior will affect
some high lady from Sicily,
so that with luck his luck will be
the luck a Spaniard should expect. 615
  What do you think of that?

DINARDA: You could
only be Toledan, I'm sure.

BERNARDO: Isn't that better than some poor
master?

DINARDA: It's thirty times as good,
  for if your master's poor, you serve 620
a knavish, roguish simpleton,
who can not tell three plates from one.

FABIO: Alright; but let us three observe
  one truth, and that is when we're in
our lodgings, we all eat together; 625
behind closed doors, no matter whether
you're lord, we're the same as we've been.

DINARDA: I agree with you.

BERNARDO: Then let's choose.
I've got three silver pieces here.

FABIO: They're all Spanish?

BERNARDO: Of course; that's clear. 630

Dinarda:	Pues bien, ¿de qué nos advierte?	
Bernardo:	Ponlos en este sombrero. El uno es real castellano, el segundo valenciano, y de Navarra el tercero; quien sacare el de Castilla, ése es rey.	635
Fabio:	Meto la mano. Yo he sacado el valenciano.	
Bernardo:	Perdiste.	
Fabio:	No es maravilla.	
Bernardo:	Saca tú.	
Dinarda:	Saco.	
Fabio:	El que queda me toca.	640
Dinarda:	Y ser dueño a mí.	
Fabio:	¿Es el de Castilla?	
Dinarda:	Sí.	
Fabio:	El premio se te conceda.	
Bernardo:	Sea en buen hora el señor.	
Fabio:	Bien está empleado en ti; que aunque me cayera a mí, no fuera el gusto mayor.	645
Bernardo:	Por muchos años y buenos seas dueño de los dos.	
Dinarda:	Para serviros ¡por Dios! puedo decir a lo menos.	650
Fabio:	Con mil razones la suerte cayó en tu gentil persona.	
Dinarda:	Quita el gentil, y perdona.	
Bernardo:	Va de nombre.	
Dinarda:	Venga.	
Bernardo:	Advierte; haste de llamar don Juan.	655
Dinarda:	¿De qué?	
Bernardo:	Escoge.	

DINARDA:	Then let's see who'll win and who'll lose.	
BERNARDO:	Drop them into this hat. There are three silver coins: now this first one is Castilian; Valencian the second; the third's from Navarre. The coin that's from Castille will be the kingmaker.	635
FABIO:	I'll put my hand in first. Valencia! That is grand.	
BERNARDO:	You lost.	
FABIO:	That doesn't surprise me.	
BERNARDO:	You try.	
DINARDA:	Here I go.	
FABIO:	The remaining one's mine.	640
DINARDA:	Then I'll be king.	
FABIO:	Did you get the Castilian coin?	
DINARDA:	It's true, I got it.	
FABIO:	Then you will be reigning!	
BERNARDO:	Long life to our new reigning king!	
FABIO:	The lottery's choice was the right one. I can tell you my delight's as great as if I'd drawn the thing.	645
BERNARDO:	May you be master of the two of us for many happy years.	
DINARDA:	By God, let me allay your fears. You know that I'll be serving you.	650
FABIO:	It's no wonder that the lot fell to this monarch of gentleness.	
DINARDA:	Gentle is the wrong word, I'd guess.	
BERNARDO:	Pick a name.	
DINARDA:	What kind of name?	
BERNARDO:	Well, would you like to be called Don Juan?	655
DINARDA:	Don Juan what?	
BERNARDO:	Who cares?	

Dinarda:	Escoger quiero; que no seré yo el primero.
Fabio:	Famoso nombre es Guzmán.
Dinarda:	Tómasele ya quienquiera. 660
Fabio:	Será Mendoza.
Dinarda:	Peor; que no hay morisco aguador que no se enmendoce.
Bernardo:	Espera. ¿Quieres Sandoval o Rojas, Manrique, Zúñiga, Lara, 665 Cárdenas, Enríquez?
Dinarda:	Para; todo el calendario arrojas. El Lara escojo no más: Don Juan de Lara es mi nombre.
Bernardo:	¡Por Dios, que vas gentilhombre! 670
Dinarda:	¿Habéis de venir detrás?
Bernardo:	Pues ¿eso dudas?
Dinarda:	Aquí se ve la industria española. ¡Hola, pajes!
Bernardo:	¡Señor!...
Dinarda:	¡Hola!
Fabio:	¡Señor!...
Dinarda:	Venid por aquí. 675

[Vanse.]
Fenisa, Celia, Lucindo y Tristán

Fenisa:	Siéntate, por vida mía.
Lucindo:	¿No ves que es tarde, mi bien?
Fenisa:	Lo que en mí es amor, también en ti ha de ser cortesía.
Lucindo:	Alégrame tanto el ver 680 tu casa tan bien compuesta, que esto tengo por más fiesta que sentarme.
Fenisa:	Hazme un placer: que lo que te diere gusto lo lleves a tu posada. 685

Dinarda:	Then I'll choose a name so grand I cannot lose.	
Fabio:	Here's a terrific name: Guzmán.	
Dinarda:	Too many people pick that one.	660
Fabio:	Mendoza, then?	
Dinarda:	That's just as bad: every Muslim water boy's had himself Mendoza-ed.	
Bernardo:	Then that's done for. There's Zúñiga? Sandoval? Manrique? Cárdenas? The list goes on: Rojas? Lara?	665
Dinarda:	Desist! Don't make me listen to them all. Lara's a fine old family. Juan de Lara's the name I'll take.	
Bernardo:	What a fine gentleman you make.	670
Dinarda:	You're committed to follow me?	
Bernardo:	You doubt we'd follow you?	
Dinarda:	You show real Spanish ingenuity. Hey! Pages!	
Bernardo:	My lord!	
Dinarda:	There, you see!	
Fabio:	Sir?	
Dinarda:	Follow me. This way, let's go.	675

[*A room in Fenisa's house*]
Fenisa, Celia, Lucindo and Tristan

Fenisa:	Sit down here. I beseech you, please.	
Lucindo:	My love, but can't you see it's late?	
Fenisa:	What with true love I supplicate, you consider mere courtesies?	
Lucindo:	I am so delighted to find your lodgings so nicely appointed. I tell you I'm not disappointed. I don't need to sit down.	680
Fenisa:	My mind is made up; please, don't disobey. If you see something you like, take it home with you.	685

LUCINDO:	No me dará gusto nada
con partido tan injusto.
¡Qué bella Cleopatra!
FENISA:	Bella,
porque amando se mató;
que ya por ti hiciera yo
lo que por Antonio ella.
LUCINDO:	¡Qué bello Narciso!
FENISA:	¡Ay, Dios!
no te mires como él;
y si has de ser tan cruel,
parezcámonos los dos,
tú en decir amores tales,
y yo en ser eco a tu llanto.
Ríeste?
LUCINDO:	De oír me espanto
que con Narciso me iguales.
Yo soy, Fenisa, más hombre,
que lindo, robusto y fuerte.
¡Oh, qué Porcia!...
FENISA:	De su muerte
no quiere amor que me asombre;
que las brasas, los enojos
con que muere, de amor loca,
si le entraron por la boca,
me entran a mí por los ojos.
LUCINDO:	¿Es éste Adonis?
FENISA:	Ansí
te imagino yo, viniendo
de caza.
LUCINDO:	¿Qué estás diciendo:
que parezco al jabalí.
Y lo que aquí cierto es,
es que eres Venus hermosa,
por cuya sangre la rosa
nació de tus blancos pies.
Aquí está la griega Elena.
FENISA:	Y el mismo París en ti.
LUCINDO:	¡Buena cama!
FENISA:	Limpia sí,
y por tu esperanza buena.
Mas ¿cómo se me olvidó
regalarte?...
LUCINDO:	Deja agora

690

695

700

705

710

715

720

LUCINDO: Why do you make
me go? Am I not here to stay?
   Lovely Cleopatra!

FENISA: You see
her as lovely because she killed
herself for love. I'd be fulfilled   690
too, if you'd be my Anthony.

LUCINDO: What a sweet Narcissus!

FENISA: Good Lord,
don't look at yourself the way he
did, and if you're going to be
cruel, let's do it in accord: 695
   you can express your love that way,
and I'll be echo to your grief.
You laugh at me?

LUCINDO: From disbelief
at the comparison. I say,
   Fenisa, I'm much more a man,   700
robust and strong. I, am no beauty.
What a Portia!

FENISA: That love and duty
killed her is no surprise. I can
   say that love drove her mad; the sighs,
the burning coals, the sharp complaints   705
that slew her through the mouth, these pains
slay me and enter through my eyes.

LUCINDO: Is this Adonis?

FENISA: That is how
I imagine you, coming from
your hunting.

LUCINDO: Where did that thought come   710
from? You think I'm a wild boar now?
   Though one thing is certainly sure:
you're a beautiful Venus, from
whose precious blood, the roses come
blooming at your feet, white and pure.   715
   What's more, you are Helen the Greek!

FENISA: Then you must be Paris, you mean.

LUCINDO: That's a fine bed.

FENISA: It is, and clean!
And well suited for what you seek.
   But how can I have been so rude?   720
May I serve you?

LUCINDO: There's no need for a

regalos.

FENISA: Celia...

CELIA: Señora...

FENISA:
[aparte a Celia] Éste ¿es mentecato?

CELIA: No.

FENISA: Pues ¿qué sientes?

CELIA: Que es discreto.

FENISA: ¿En qué lo has visto?

CELIA: En que ya 725
viene sin cadena acá.

FENISA: No lo advertí, te prometo.
   Quedo, sin cadena viene.
El es bellaco.

CELIA: Y ¡qué tal!
Lo que intentas saldrá mal. 730

FENISA: ¿Por qué?

CELIA: Gran defensa tiene.

FENISA: Engañar, Celia, un cuitado
barbitonto, boquinecio,
no fuera hazaña de precio
ni digna de humor taimado; 735
   pasmar un ingenio agudo
es lo que se ha de estimar.
¿Cadena sabe guardar?

CELIA: Y que se la pesques dudo.

FENISA: Estudiar con más cuidado; 740
que engañar a un cauteloso
es pleito dificultoso
que hace estudiar al letrado.
   Abreme esa librería
de engaños, trazas y enredos. 745

LUCINDO:
[aparte a Tristán] ¿Qué temes?

TRISTÁN: Tengo mil miedos
a tu humor y cortesía.
   ¡Guarda, que te ha de engañar!

LUCINDO: ¿En qué, pues tienes el oro?

	lot of fussing.	
FENISA:	Celia!	
CELIA:	Señora...	
FENISA: *[aside to Celia]*	Is this man a dummy, or crude?	
CELIA:	No.	
FENISA:	Well, what is it then?	
CELIA:	He's clever.	
FENISA:	What makes you say that?	
CELIA:	I'll explain: he's come here without his gold chain.	725
FENISA:	You're right. I don't think I have ever thought of that. The chain's gone. Take care! He must be a scoundrel.	
CELIA:	You bet. What you hope for you'll never get.	730
FENISA:	Why?	
CELIA:	His defense is everywhere.	
FENISA:	To deceive, Celia, a drunk, blind, lollygagging credulous lout is nothing to be proud about, and no proof of a clever mind. Pulling wool over clever eyes that is something worthy of pride. You say his chain is locked inside?	735
CELIA:	If you catch it, I'll be surprised.	
FENISA:	I'll have to study with more care, for deceiving a cautious man is a tough job, and needs a plan a genius would have to prepare. Open that bookshelf of deceits and tricks and stratagems and wiles.	740 745
LUCINDO: *[aside to Tristan]*	What are you afraid of?	
TRISTAN:	Your smiles worry me, and your sweet conceits. She's likely to fool you: watch out!	
LUCINDO:	How can she? The gold's in your care.	

FENISA:
[aparte]   Circe, tu deidad imploro.   750

CELIA: ¿El cebo quieres gastar?

FENISA: Vé por el primer anzuelo.
[alto]   Traigan aquí colación.

[Vase Celia.]
                       Siéntate, amores.

LUCINDO:
[aparte a Tristán]   Que son
                términos nobles recelo.   755
                    ¿Qué he de perder en sentarme?

[Siéntanse en dos sillas.]

TRISTÁN:
[aparte a su amo]   ¿Ya te asientas?

LUCINDO: Calla, loco.

FENISA: Háblame, mi vida, un poco;
                que está en tu mano alegrarme.

LUCINDO: ¿Qué te diré?

FENISA: Que me quieres,   760
                aunque mientas.

LUCINDO: No estoy muerto;
                mas bien te quiero, por cierto.

FENISA: ¿Por cierto? ¡oh, qué lindo eres!
                    ¿Qué es *por cierto*? ¿Tú eres, di,
                español?

LUCINDO: Pues ¿no lo ves?   765

FENISA: El *por cierto* no lo es;
                el talle y la lengua sí.
                    Yo aseguro que en mil años
                no ha pasado otro *por cierto*
                a Italia.

LUCINDO: Que soy, te advierto,   770
                nuevo por reinos extraños.

FENISA: Bien pareces de Valencia.

LUCINDO: Somos muy tiernos allá.

FENISA: El *por cierto* lo dirá.
                Jura luego *en mi conciencia*,   775
                  y queriendo encarecer
                lo que a darte gusto cuadre,

FENISA:
[Aside]   Oh Circe, goddess, hear my prayer.   750

CELIA: That's why you bring all this bait out?

FENISA: You go and get out the first hook.
                           Would you bring the refreshments, please?

[Celia exits.]

FENISA: Sit down, my love; be seated.

LUCINDO:
[Aside to Tristan]   These
                  words come out of a courtly book.   755
                     What can I lose in sitting down?

[The two sit down on chairs.]

TRISTAN:
[Aside to Lucindo]   You're sitting down?

LUCINDO: Shut up, you ass!

FENISA: Come talk to me, love, help me pass
                     the time; come and erase my frown.

LUCINDO: What shall I say?

FENISA: Say you love me,   760
                   though you may lie.

LUCINDO: My thoughts are pure.
                   I do love you, for certain sure.

FENISA: *Certain sure!* What gentility!
                     What's this *For certain sure*? Are you
                   a real Spaniard?

LUCINDO: What do you mean?   765

FENISA: That *For certain sure* does not seem
                     so; the good looks and tongue ring true.
                       In the last thousand years or more
                     not one *For certain sure* has made
                     it to Italy.

LUCINDO: I've not strayed,   770
                   you see, from my homeland before.

FENISA: That sounds like a Valencian text.

LUCINDO: We're very tender people there.

FENISA: *For certain sure* makes me aware
                     of that. *By my conscience* comes next.   775
                       And if you want to win the day
                     and get what you want with real skill,

di, *por vida* de mi madre,
que bien será menester.
    Vesme estar desatinada, 780
y cuando desto te advierto,
¡me respondes un *por cierto*
envuelto en agua rosada!
    No, español, yo no te agrado,
o tú quieres bien allá, 785
y ausencia pena te da.
Oye: ¿estás enamorado?
    Por mis ojos, por los tuyos,
por los de amor, aunque ciegos,
que te muevas a mis ruegos 790
y me encarezcas los suyos.
    ¿Son negros, garzos o azules?
¿Qué pelo, qué humor, qué talle?
¿Pensaste agora en su calle?
Ea, no lo disimules; 795
    en Valencia estás agora.
¿Qué hay nuevo en Valencia? Diga.

TRISTÁN:
[aparte]   ¡Oh socarrona!

LUCINDO: Mi amiga,
toda Valencia os adora.
    Esto hay de nuevo; y si allá 800
algún gusto me entretuvo,
hasta veros vida tuvo,
y porque os vi, muerto está.
    Una mujer me quería
dar a su madre por suegra, 805
entre blanca y pelinegra,
y el ingenio argentería.
    Enviámonos las almas
en papeles cuatro meses,
con requiebros portugueses, 810
trayendo este amor en palmas.
    Vila en una huerta un día,
más cerca, menos hermosa;
habléla, y la hallé enfadosa;
toquéla, y estaba fría. 815
    Salí con menos pasión;
y ofreciéndose esta ausencia,
no dejé cosa en Valencia,
fuera de la obligación.

FENISA: ¡Ay de mí! ¡Cómo era cierto! 820
¿Que hombre que a mí me agradase,
otra amase, y me tratase
con traición?

	say *By my mother's life*, which will	
	certainly help you get your way.	
	You see me standing here excited,	780
	telling you this, and even so,	
	this *For certain sure* is a blow;	
	and you think I will be delighted?	
	No, Spaniard, you must not love me,	
	or else you have a love back there,	785
	and absence causes you despair.	
	Is this another love I see?	
	By my eyes, or if not, by yours,	
	by the eyes of love, though he's blind,	
	give in to my pleas, speak your mind	790
	and say what's so great about hers.	
	Are her eyes black, or slate, or blue?	
	And her hair? Her figure? What gives	
	you that smile? Thinking where she lives?	
	Don't kid me: I know what you do:	795
	Your head is in Valencia; tell	
	me what's new in Valencia then.	
TRISTAN:		
[aside]	What a trickster.	
LUCINDO:	All of the men	
	of my Valencia love you well.	
	That's what's new. And if back there some	800
	trifling pleasure did turn my head,	
	now that I've seen you, that love's dead;	
	since I've seen you to life I've come.	
	Some woman wanted to give me	
	her mother for mother-in-law.	805
	White skin and raven hair I saw,	
	and cash for ingenuity.	
	Four months the love letters we sent,	
	in paper wrapping up our souls;	
	playing out all the lovesick roles,	810
	writing down what we thought we meant.	
	In a garden we met one day;	
	I saw her more closely, less pretty.	
	I spoke to her; it was a pity.	
	I touched her; she was cold as clay.	815
	I left her there with far less passion,	
	and when I got this chance to leave	
	Valencia I did; I don't grieve	
	for people there in any fashion.	
FENISA:	Alas! I was right. It is true!	820
	That a man I want to love me	
	should treat me with such treachery!	

LUCINDO:	Oye.	
FENISA:	Hasme muerto.	
LUCINDO:	¿Lloras? El lienzo desvía.	
TRISTÁN: *[aparte]*	¿Hay semejante bellaca?	825
LUCINDO:	El sol de esas nieblas sacad, regalada prenda mía. No me des esos enojos.	
FENISA:	A fe que tiene él acá prendas que trujo de allá.	830
LUCINDO:	Tormento me dan tus ojos, verdades me hacen decir, mil jarros de agua me dan.	
FENISA:	¿Dónde las prendas están?	
TRISTÁN: *[aparte]*	¿Hay tan notable fingir?	835
FENISA:	A fe que era la cadena, por eso se la quitó; no lloro sin causa yo.	
LUCINDO:	¿La cadena te dio pena?	
TRISTÁN: *[aparte]*	El se ablanda: ¡vive Dios, que la cadena se anega!	840
LUCINDO:	Oye, mi vida, y sosiega.	
TRISTÁN: *[aparte]*	Cadena, volved por vos.	
LUCINDO:	Como no traigo dinero, hasta vender, la envié con Tristán...	845
TRISTÁN:	Yo la llevé en casa de un caballero.	
FENISA:	Y ¿qué dinero te dio?	
TRISTÁN:	No estaba en casa, y dejéla.	
FENISA: *[aparte]*	El picarón me desvela; pero déstos pesco yo. ¿El dinero te ha faltado? Celia...	850
CELIA: *[dentro]*	Señora...	

LUCINDO:	Hang on!	
FENISA:	Do you know what you do?	
LUCINDO:	Tears? Put your handkerchief away.	
TRISTAN: [aside]	This kind of trickery's unique.	825
LUCINDO:	Let your sunny complexion peek through the clouds. Love, can't you be gay? Don't destroy me with your sad sighs.	
FENISA:	I'll bet he has a souvenir of that Valencian woman here.	830
LUCINDO:	I am tormented by your eyes. They torture me to speak the truth. I weep, whether I would or not.	
FENISA:	Where have you put the things you brought?	
TRISTAN: [aside]	What perfect deceit! How uncouth!	835
FENISA:	You must be talking of the chain, and that's why you put it away. You see what makes me cry today.	
LUCINDO:	The chain is what gives you such pain?	
TRISTAN: [aside]	Good God, I think he's giving in, and the chain is as good as gone!	840
FENISA:	Listen, my love: you must be calm.	
TRISTAN: [aside]	Chain, you must fight to save your skin.	
LUCINDO:	Since I have no money with me until my cargo's sold, Tristan took it.	845
TRISTAN:	I left it with a man who keeps things with security.	
FENISA:	And I assume he gave you money?	
TRISTAN:	He'd gone out, so I left it there.	
FENISA: [aside]	What an easy catch. Let him dare to try to pull anything funny. Did all your money disappear? Celia!	850
CELIA: [inside]	My lady.	

FENISA: ¿No vienes?

[Sale Celia con dos criados, con una conserva, paño al hombro, taza y salva.]

CELIA:	Aquí la conserva tienes.	
FENISA:	Come, mi vida, un bocado.	855
	Vé, Celia, y sácame aquí	
	el escritorio pequeño	

[Vase Celia.]

Melindres come, mi dueño,
del alma que vive en ti;
  come, que ya eres señor 860
desta casa.

TRISTÁN:
[aparte] ¡Qué criados
tan bien puestos, tan honrados!

LUCINDO:
*[aparte a su
criado]* Tristán...

TRISTÁN: Señor...

LUCINDO: Grande error
es no creer que esta dama
es persona principal. 865

TRISTÁN: Hasta agora pensé mal
de sus obras y su fama;
  digo que pido perdón.

FENISA: ¿No bebes?

LUCINDO: Denme a beber.

TRISTÁN:
[aparte a su amo] Necio has estado en comer. 870

LUCINDO: Calla, que ha sido invención;
  que el bocado que cogí
le guardé en el lienzo.

TRISTÁN: Bien.

LUCINDO: Y luego fingí también
que le comí.

TRISTÁN: ¿Bebes?

LUCINDO: Sí. 875

TRISTÁN: No bebas.

LUCINDO: ¿Qué puede haber

FENISA: Where've you been?

[Celia enters with two servants, with a bowl of sweetmeats, a towel on her shoulder, a cup and tray.]

CELIA: Look, here are the sweets I've brought in.

FENISA: Come try a taste of this, my dear. 855
    Celia, bring over here the small
secretary; I need it please.

[Exit Celia.]

Master, try these bonbons. Don't tease.
My soul is in them, one and all.
    Eat up, you know you are the lord 860
of this house.

TRISTAN:
[aside]   What fine servants she
has; they're as honored as can be.

LUCINDO:
[aside] Tristan...

TRISTAN: Sir...

LUCINDO: You must behave toward
her as to a most noble dame,
or a lady of great repute. 865

TRISTAN: I haven't yet. I'll not refute
that I've thought badly of her fame.
    You must forgive me if you can.

FENISA: You're not drinking?

LUCINDO: Please. Let me drink.

TRISTAN:
[aside to
Lucindo] That was a foolish move I think. 870

LUCINDO: Shut up; that's all part of my plan.
    I palmed the candy that I took
and hid it in this cloth.

TRISTAN: Right.

LUCINDO: I only pretended to bite
on it.

TRISTAN: But you are drinking.

LUCINDO: Look. 875

TRISTAN: Don't touch that drink.

LUCINDO: There's a surprise

en el vino?

TRISTÁN: Mucho mal.

FENISA:
[aparte] No ha comido. ¿Hay cosa igual?
Demonio debe de ser.

LUCINDO: Agua bebo.

FENISA: Agua le den. 880

LUCINDO:
[aparte] En agua no habrá sospecha.

FENISA:
[aparte] Este mi engaño sospecha,
y hele de engañar más bien.

[Celia, con un escritorio pequeño y criados]

CELIA: Ya el escritorio está aquí.

FENISA: Llégamele luego acá. 885

CELIA: ¿Tienes la llave?

FENISA: Aquí está;
que en la manga la metí.

LUCINDO: ¿Qué tienes ahí?

FENISA: Estos días
muy desproveído está;
bagatelas son, que allá 890
soléis llamar niñerías.
Estos son guantes: bien puedes
tomar estos cuatro pares.

LUCINDO: ¿Son de ámbar?

FENISA: Sí; no repares.

LUCINDO: Hácesme dos mil mercedes. 895

FENISA: Pastillas has menester;
no son limpias las posadas;
seis docenas extremadas
me envió una monja ayer.
Toma, en ese papel van. 900
¿Qué tengo yo más que darte?

LUCINDO:
[aparte a él] ¿Con qué puedo yo pagarte?
Perdidos vamos, Tristán.

TRISTÁN: En extraña confusión
te ha puesto aquesta mujer. 905

FENISA: Medias solía tener

	in the wine?	
TRISTAN:	You never can tell.	
FENISA: [aside]	He avoids food and drink as well. Is he the devil in disguise?	
LUCINDO:	I would drink water.	
FENISA:	Bring a cup.	880
LUCINDO: [aside]	At least water can't make me sick.	
FENISA: [aside]	I think he's caught on to my trick. But my tricks are not all used up.	

[Celia, with a small secretary desk]

CELIA:	The secretary I believe you wanted.	
FENISA:	Put it over there.	885
CELIA:	Have you a key?	
FENISA:	I put it where I'd not misplace it: in my sleeve.	
LUCINDO:	What have you got in there?	
FENISA:	You came at a bad time, there's hardly any thing: a few toys, trinkets, not many. Trifles might be a better name. Here are some gloves. Why don't you take this pair? Here, you can take all four.	890
LUCINDO:	They seem like amber.	
FENISA:	Yes. Take more.	
LUCINDO:	You do too much, love, for my sake.	895
FENISA:	Take some incense to drive away the smell from those lodgings of yours. A nun sent six dozen of hers over to the house yesterday. Here, I wrapped them up in this paper. Now, tell me what else I can do.	900
LUCINDO: [aside]	How can I ever repay you? Tristan: now we'll never escape her.	
TRISTAN:	I can see you feel like a fool with this strange generosity.	905
FENISA:	These stockings are good quality;	

      de Nápoles.

LUCINDO: Buenas son.

FENISA: Tristán…

TRISTÁN: Señora…

FENISA: Aquí van
dos pares.

TRISTÁN: Guárdete Dios.

FENISA: También las hay para vos;   910
tomad.

LUCINDO:
[aparte]   ¿Qué es esto, Tristán?

TRISTÁN: ¿Qué ha de ser? Indias cifradas
en escritorios de amor.

LUCINDO: Hácesnos tanto favor,
que están las manos turbadas.   915

FENISA: Toma este bolsillo.

LUCINDO: Beso
tus manos. Escucha.

FENISA: Di.

LUCINDO: Dineros suenan aquí,
y lo mismo dice el peso.

FENISA: Cien escudos hallarás   920
mientras no tienes dinero
y por lo que yo te quiero,
que vayas pidiendo más;
 que cuando muchos te sobren,
me los pagarás, si quieres.   925

LUCINDO: Hija de Alejandro eres.

TRISTÁN: Yo te juro que se cobren.

Liseo, Estacio y un escudero

ESCUDERO:
*[aparte a un
criado]*   ¿Qué pez es éste?

LISEO: No sé.

ESTACIO: Un mercader valenciano.

LISEO: Ganando va por la mano.   930

CELIA: Perderáse por el pie.

ESTACIO: Pues que Fenisa le fía,

	they're from Naples.	
Lucindo:	They're beautiful.	
Fenisa:	Tristan.	
Tristan:	Ma'am.	
Fenisa:	These will look good on you.	
Tristan:	May God grant you his reward.	
Fenisa:	And this pair is for you, my lord. Take them.	910
Lucindo: *[aside]*	What can this be, Tristan?	
Tristan:	What can it be? She has the treasure of the Indies locked in this chest.	
Lucindo:	Such fine gifts leave me all distressed. You do us favors without measure.	915
Fenisa:	Take this purse.	
Lucindo:	I kiss your hands. Wait a moment.	
Fenisa:	Why, what do you fear?	
Lucindo:	I can hear coins clinking in here; lots of them, to judge by the weight.	
Fenisa:	A hundred scudos you will find, to tide you over while you're low. It's because I love you, you know. If you need, there's more, I won't mind. Some day, when you have coins galore, you can pay me back if you want.	920 925
Lucindo:	You must be Alexander's aunt!	
Tristan:	She'll get them back, and many more.	

Liseo, Estacio and a squire

Squire:	What kind of fish is this?	
Liseo:	Beats me!	
Estacio:	A merchant, from some Spanish land.	
Liseo:	She's dragging him down by the hand.	930
Celia:	He'll fall hand over foot, you'll see.	
Estacio:	If he gives Fenisa her head,	

hipotecado tendrá.

LUCINDO: Mi señora, tarde es ya,
y también la hacienda mía 935
quiere un poco de cuidado.

FENISA: El cielo vaya contigo.
¿Haste de acordar, amigo,
del alma que me has llevado?

LUCINDO: Cadenas de obligaciones 940
me acordarán mi ventura,
pues sin las de tu hermosura,
en las que llevo me pones.
    Pienso que sabrá pagarte,
aunque si esta nave fuera 945
de oro puro, no pudiera
deste bien mínima parte.
    ¡Ojalá fueran sus jarcias
cuerdas de perlas de Oriente,
. . . . 950
. . . .
    El corredor de su popa
fuera de diamantes hecho,
de historias varias el techo,
del pincel mejor de Europa; 955
    y para arrastrar en faldas
de tu ropa ricas telas,
fueran brocado sus velas,
sus árboles de esmeraldas
    la jarela de cadenas, 960
los trinquetes y mesanas
de rubíes como granas,
y de coral las entenas!
    ésta te diera en presente,
y en la mitad del fogón 965
pusiera mi corazón,
porque ardiera eternamente.

FENISA: Guárdeteme Dios mil años.
¡Hola! Acompañalde todos.

LUCINDO:
[aparte a Tristán] ¿Qué es esto?

TRISTÁN: Notables modos... 970

LUCINDO: ¿De qué?

TRISTÁN: De amor o de engaños.

	he'll be mortgaged up to his ears.	
LUCINDO:	Lady, it's growing late. My fears for my belongings, as I've said, require me to depart, you know.	935
FENISA:	May Heaven prosper what you do. You are aware, my friend, that you take my soul wherever you go.	
LUCINDO:	The debt I owe you is the chain that keeps my good luck in my mind; without your beauty's chains I'd find that debt would equally constrain. I know I'll figure how to pay you back; though even if this ship were solid gold, and I to strip it for you, I could not repay all I owe. How I wish the rigging were draped with strings of precious pearls! . . . .* I wish the afterdeck were hung with diamonds shining bright as flames and canvases by famous names, the best that Europe ever sung. And so that you would be enthralled by gowns of finest fabrics made, I wish the sails were rich brocade and that the masts were emerald; I wish the lines were jeweled strings, the foremast and the mizzen mast were from the brightest rubies cast, the yardarms strung with coral rings. These presents I would give to you and on the galley hearth I'd lay my heart; and burning, it would say my love will be forever true.	940 945 950 955 960 965
FENISA:	May God keep you for me forever. Hello! You two accompany him.	
LUCINDO:	What's this?	
TRISTAN:	A fine strategy.	970
LUCINDO:	For what?	
TRISTAN:	For love or being clever.	

---

*Two verses are missing from this quatrain/*redondilla*.

| LUCINDO: | Yo presumo que es amor; |
| | que amor en obras se ve. |

| TRISTÁN: | En el fin te lo diré, |
| | que allá se sabrá mejor. | 975 |

Vanse Lucindo, Tristán, el escudero y los criados.

| CELIA: | A mucho te has atrevido. |

| FENISA: | Ésta es ganancia segura. |

| CELIA: | Así Dios me dé ventura, |
| | que pienso que te ha entendido. |

| FENISA: | Pues ¿qué gusto puede haber | 980 |
| | como avisar y engañar? |

El capitán Osorio, Dinarda, en hábito de hombre, Bernardo y Fabio

| OSORIO: | ¿Puedo entrar? |

| FENISA: | Puedes entrar. |

| OSORIO: | Un huésped traigo a comer. |

| DINARDA: | Vuesamerced, mi señora, |
| | me tenga por su criado. | 985 |

| FENISA: | Seáis, señor, bien llegado. |
| | ¿Es de España? |

| OSORIO: | Y llega agora. |

| FENISA: | ¿Caballero? |

| OSORIO: | ¿No lo ves? |

| FENISA: | ¿El nombre? |

| OSORIO: | Don Juan de Lara. |

| FENISA: | Buena cara. |

| OSORIO: | Linda cara. | 990 |

DINARDA:	Partí de España habrá un mes,
	llegué a Sicilia en el día
	de mi vida más dichoso,
	pues veo ese rostro hermoso.

| FENISA: | Estimo la cortesía. | 995 |
| | ¿A qué venís? |

DINARDA:	A servir
	al rey con los alimentos
	de padre y madre avarientos,
	hasta quererse morir.

LUCINDO:	For love, then. At least I assume it's for love. Her actions will tell.	
TRISTAN:	I'll tell you what it is I smell when we're safely out of her room.	975

[Exit Lucindo, Tristan, the squire and the servants.]

CELIA:	It seems to me you've risked a lot.	
FENISA:	Wait 'til you see how much I get.	
CELIA:	I hope good luck is with you yet, for I think he's wise to your plot.	
FENISA:	The pleasure of deceit is fine when I deceive with a good clue.	980

Captain Osorio, Dinarda dressed as a man; Bernardo and Fabio

OSORIO:	May I come in?	
FENISA:	Of course, please do.	
OSORIO:	I've brought a guest with me to dine.	
DINARDA:	Your grace, my lady, I obey your every word; I'm here to serve.	985
FENISA:	Sir, this is more than I deserve. Is he from Spain?	
OSORIO:	Just came today.	
FENISA:	And a gentleman?	
OSORIO:	His clothes show him to be.	
FENISA:	What's his name?	
OSORIO:	Don Juan de Lara.	
FENISA:	He's a handsome one.	990
DINARDA:	I sailed from Spain a month ago. The day I came to Sicily is of my life the happiest; Seeing your lovely face I'm blessed.	
FENISA:	I thank you for the courtesy. What brings you to our shore?	995
DINARDA:	Well, I brought the king some goods that are so anxious for a new home, I know that if they have to wait they'll die.	

FENISA: Dios los despache a su cielo. 1000
DINARDA: Pajes...
BERNARDO: Señor...
DINARDA: Responded.
FABIO: Amén.
DINARDA: Notable merced
me hiciera.
FENISA:
[aparte] ¡Gentil mozuelo!
DINARDA: Llegué a un corro de soldados,
hallé al señor capitán, 1005
que es de mi tierra, y que están
deudos con deudas casados;
  ofrecióme su posada,
y para mayor favor
me trujo aquí.
FENISA: Obliga a amor 1010
ver vuestra persona honrada;
  no hay cartas más afectivas,
para que el favor se halle,
que la buena cara y talle.
OSORIO: Comamos, Celia, ansí vivas. 1015
CELIA: Ya está todo prevenido.
BERNARDO:
[aparte a su
compañero] Fabio...
FABIO: ¿Qué?
BERNARDO: Ya la picaña
se inclina al humor de España.
FABIO: Hablándose están de oído.
BERNARDO: En entrándose, me llego. 1020
FABIO: ¿A quién?
BERNARDO: A Francisquina.
FABIO: Mas ¿qué tenemos mohina?
BERNARDO: Aqueso niego y reniego;
  que está la mujer por mía
desde que el umbral pisé. 1025
OSORIO:
[a Fenisa] ¿Ya me dais celos?

FENISA:	May God dispatch them: one, two, three!	1000
DINARDA:	Pages...	
BERNARDO:	My lord...	
DINARDA:	What do you say?	
FABIO:	Amen.	
DINARDA:	I require this display of breeding.	
FENISA: [aside]	What a youth I see!	
DINARDA:	In a group of soldiers I saw the good Captain, who emigrated from my city, and who's related somehow to some cousins-in-law. His lodgings he offered to share, and to honor me further still, he brought me here.	1005
FENISA:	Your honor will make my heart love you, I declare. Love letters convey less emotion, and commitment comes less from books than from a good build and nice looks.	1010
OSORIO:	Let's eat now, Celia; that's my notion.	1015
CELIA:	It's all ready for savoring.	
BERNARDO:	Fabio.	
FABIO:	What?	
BERNARDO:	Take a look at how she's warming up to Spaniards now.	
FABIO:	Just look at those two whispering.	
BERNARDO:	When they go in I'll make my move.	1020
FABIO:	On whom?	
BERNARDO:	On Francisca, that's who.	
FABIO:	You'd cut me out? That's what you'd do?	
BERNARDO:	And what are you trying to prove? Not a damn thing! That girl was mine from when I first came in the door.	1025
OSORIO: [to Fenisa]	You make me jealous?	

Fenisa:	¿De qué? Vos me enseñáis cortesía.
Osorio:	Vamos, que yo gusto mucho que honréis al señor don Juan.
Dinarda: [aparte]	Tiernas las hembras están. 1030
Fenisa: [aparte a ella]	Escucha, Celia.
Celia:	Ya escucho.
Fenisa:	¡Notable español!
Celia:	Gallardo.
Fenisa:	En mi vida tuve amor, pero ya fuera mejor no haberle visto.
Celia:	Eso aguardo. 1035
Fenisa:	De Sevilla dice que es.
Celia:	Es gente en extremo airosa.
Fenisa:	Fuera de la cara hermosa, me matan piernas y pies.
Celia:	Tienes lindo gusto.
Fenisa:	El mío 1040 este despejo procura: que del hombre la hermosura consiste en piernas y brío.
Osorio:	Venid, don Juan, a comer.
Dinarda:	Pajes...
Bernardo:	Señor...
Dinarda: [aparte a los pajes]	¡Bueno va! 1045
Bernardo:	¿Pica?
Dinarda:	Picada está ya... aunque fue sin alfiler.

FENISA: Me? What for?
You're showing me how to act fine.

OSORIO: Come on; you know how much it cheers
me to see you honor Don Juan.

DINARDA:
[aside] Say, these women are really fun! 1030

FENISA:
[aside] Listen, Celia.

CELIA: I am all ears.

FENISA: He's Spanish to the core.

CELIA: And cute!

FENISA: I've never truly loved as yet;
and now I'm sorry that I met
him at all.

CELIA: That I won't dispute. 1035

FENISA: He says that he comes from Seville.

CELIA: His prideful bearing is a treat.

FENISA: His face is handsome, and his feet
are cute, but his legs really kill.

CELIA: You have perfect taste.

FENISA: I decide 1040
if a man's goodlooking by two
things, which I recommend to you:
his good legs and his sense of pride.

OSORIO: It's time to eat, Don Juan; come look.

DINARDA: Pages...

BERNARDO: My lord...

DINARDA:
*[aside to his
pages]* It's all first rate! 1045

BERNARDO: Did she take it?

DINARDA: She took the bait,
but hasn't taken the hook.

Jornada Segunda

Lucindo y Tristán

LUCINDO:	No te congoje, Tristán,	
	que entre y salga quien quisiere;	
	parientes suyos serán.	1050
TRISTÁN:	Por mí, sea lo que fuere	
	este español capitán.	
	Bien sé que en un mes y más	
	que ninguna cosa das,	
	y mil regalos recibes;	1055
	seguro de engaños vives,	
	pero de amor no lo estás.	
	Quien no da no tiene acción	
	a pedir celos, ni hacer	
	de agravios demostración;	1060
	sólo el dar en la mujer	
	alcanza jurisdicción.	
	Ése al injusto adulterio	
	del trato noble y sencillo	
	puede llamar vituperio	1065
	porque tiene horca y cuchillo	
	con su mero y mixto imperio.	
	Mas has de advertir también	
	que la vas queriendo bien;	
	y aunque no te cuesta nada,	1070
	¡bueno quedas, si se enfada	
	y te trata con desdén!	
	Que por ver que la desvía	
	de tu gusto otro interés	
	que enriquecerla porfía,	1075
	lo que no has dado en un mes,	
	vendrás a darle en un día.	
LUCINDO:	No pienso yo que Fenisa,	
	Tristán, por otro me deje;	
	que eso de interés es risa.	1080
TRISTÁN:	Amor, obstinado hereje,	
	las mismas verdades pisa.	
	El que en mujer se confía,	
	lejos está de discreto.	
LUCINDO:	No ha sido la culpa mía;	1085
	es la hermosura, en efeto,	
	una breve tiranía.	
	Todos los sabios de Grecia,	
	que vieran que una mujer	
	cuanto es interés desprecia	1090

Act II

[Lucindo's room]
Lucindo and Tristan

LUCINDO: Tristan, you should not be upset
to see so many come and go:
they're all her relatives, I know. 1050

TRISTAN: Some of them may be, but I'll bet
the Spanish Captain isn't though.
   I know that the five weeks that you've
not given anything to her
and she's showered you with gifts prove 1055
you're safe from traps; but don't infer
that you're likewise from love secure.
   If you don't give, you have no right
to be jealous, or to complain
at some real or imagined slight; 1060
you get title by paying plain
cash. Without presents love takes flight.
   Once you give her gifts you can make
the case that her honor is fake,
that this traffic's adultery. 1065
Give her something, then you can take
your vengeance with impunity.
   You get in trouble when you fall
in love; and you have, I'm afraid.
In that case, though you haven't paid 1070
her, one rough word from her and all
your defenses will be mislaid.
   For as soon as you see her turn
her head from you to follow some
other man with more cash, you'll come 1075
to give in one day what you earn
in a month. That's how you will learn!

LUCINDO: I don't think that Fenisa would
leave me, Tristan, for someone else;
for money, I don't think she could. 1080

TRISTAN: What a stubborn heretic: good
old love, the same lie always tells.
   Any man who chooses to trust
a woman is far from discreet.

LUCINDO: The fault has not been mine: you must 1085
know it's beauty's fault; beauty's just
tyranny, designed to defeat
   a man. All the sages of Greece,
if they'd see some woman disdain
any interest in worldly gain 1090

>   con hidalgo proceder,
>   y que no es fea ni es necia;
>   Diógenes o Timón,
>   que jamás trató con gente,
>   que vieran tanta afición,   1095
>   se rindieran tiernamente
>   por amor u obligación.
>   Yo me resistí unos días;
>   mas viendo tantas verdades,
>   rendí mis vanas porfías.   1100

TRISTÁN: Con razón me persüades.

LUCINDO: Venció las sospechas mías.

TRISTÁN: Al principio fue el error.

LUCINDO: No le pude hacer mayor
            que no retirarme luego.   1105

TRISTÁN: Estando cerca del fuego,
            era forzoso el calor.

LUCINDO: Si con la razón se mide,
            no lo será que te asombre;
            que ¿cómo, hasta que le olvide,   1110
            ha de retirarse un hombre
            de una mujer que no pide?
               Digo, que si a mí me hicieren
            regalos, mientras me dieren
            y de pedirme se extrañen,   1115
            doy licencia que me engañen
            cuantas mujeres quisieren.

TRISTÁN: No reprehendo el entrar
            en su casa, pues no hay dar
            el valor de un alfiler...   1120

LUCINDO: Pues ¿qué dices?

TRISTÁN: El querer.

LUCINDO: No lo he podido excusar.
               Es bellísima, Tristán,
            y es justo que consideres
            partes que en el alma están.   1125
            La hermosura en las mujeres
            es gracia que a todos dan.
               El villano y el señor
            ven la hermosura exterior;
            la más cuerda o la más loca,   1130
            para cualquiera se toca,
            pues ha de verla en rigor.
               Sola una vez la hermosura

	with scorn, if they were not plain,
	ugly, dimwitted or obese,
	even wise old Diogenes,
	so rare were good women like these,
	that if they saw this concentration 1095
	of virtue, would fall on their knees
	from love, or other obligation.
	I held out for many a day,
	but these truths were so manifest,
	my objections melted away. 1100

TRISTAN: With all these reasons I'm impressed.

LUCINDO: My suspicions are put to rest.

TRISTAN: From the first I made a mistake.

LUCINDO: All these good arguments require
me to change and make a clean break. 1105

TRISTAN: If you stand that close to the fire,
then the heat will make you perspire.

LUCINDO: If you follow reason's commands
you won't be surprised by this one.
For until she washes her hands 1110
of him, how can any man run
from a girl who makes no demands?
   I can tell you that just as long
as women give me gifts, and they
keep on, and I don't have to pay, 1115
then the woman can do no wrong:
I'm pleased to be deceived this way.

TRISTAN: I don't reprehend you for going
to her house, though you may be owing
her some day the price of a hook. 1120

LUCINDO: How's that again?

TRISTAN: I mean love.

LUCINDO: Look,
I can't help if my love is showing.
   Tristan, the woman's beautiful:
you have to take into account
the things of which her soul is full. 1125
In women, beauty is the fount
of grace which makes them beautiful.
   The noble lord and common man
see exterior loveliness:
wild or pure, a woman will stress 1130
her looks with makeup if she can,
since attracting men is her plan.
   And beauty pulls you off the track

```
                    goza el que llevó la palma;
                    lo que es nuevo, poco dura,                          1135
                    lo que es secreto es el alma;
                    ésta el amor asegura.
                       Ésta se muestra en el trato,
                    déste nace mi afición;
                    ya no hay amar con recato;                           1140
                    que tras tanta obligación
                    fuera bajeza de ingrato.
                       Yo la adoro, porque sé
                    que es verdadero su amor.
                    Ya por esta puerta entré:                            1145
                    de interés competidor
                    no es bien que celoso esté.
                       Este español capitán
                    y otros que entran en su casa,
                    ninguna pena me dan,                                 1150
                    porque es cosa que no pasa
                    de conversación, Tristán,
                       fuera de que yo he venido,
                    y me iré cuando quisiere,
                    gustoso y entretenido,                               1155
                    adonde verla no espere,
                    y el ausencia cause olvido.
                       Contaré en Valencia el cuento
                    a los amigos y damas
                    con grande gusto y contento...                       1160
```

TRISTÁN: Con razón cuento le llamas.

LUCINDO: ¿Llamaron?

TRISTÁN: Sí.

LUCINDO: Gente siento.

Celia, con manto; el escudero con un tabaque cubierto con un tafetán

CELIA: ¡Qué descuidado estarás
                deste visita!

LUCINDO: Jamás,
                Celia, lo estoy de tu dueño.   1165

CELIA: Allá nos quitas el sueño,
                y acá sin memoria estás;
                    mas que, ¿agora te levantas?

LUCINDO: No duermen los mercaderes
                tanto, y más con penas tantas.   1170

CELIA: ¿Penas, si adorado eres?

> only the first time; that's a fact.
> Newness has but a passing role. 1135
> What's hidden away is the soul:
> that is what will truly attract.
>   That behavior makes manifest;
> that's where my love was first begot.
> My love must be richly expressed. 1140
> What with her gifts, if I did not
> I would be an ingrate, at best.
>   Those are the reasons I adore
> her, for I know her love is true.
> I love her, I've opened that door. 1145
> I'm not suspicious; I tell you
> money's not what these deeds are for.
>   I'm not jealous of any man,
> like the Spanish Captain who goes
> to her house, because my heart knows 1150
> that this is nothing other than
> social conversation, Tristan.
>   Besides, I'm just a visitor
> here, and one day soon I'll be gone,
> happy, delighted to the core, 1155
> to where I'll never look upon
> her again, or think of her more.
>   Once home, the story I'll relate
> to all the ladies and my friends,
> with joy and delight, both intense. 1160

TRISTAN: It's a story, at any rate.

LUCINDO: That's a knock.

TRISTAN: Yes.

LUCINDO: Don't make them wait.

Celia in a shawl; the Squire with a cloth-wrapped package

CELIA: It seems we've caught you unprepared
for our visit.

LUCINDO: You'll not see me
unprepared to show courtesy 1165
to your mistress.

CELIA: How have you dared
to sleep late, when it's your fault we
cannot sleep? You're wakened just now?

LUCINDO: Merchants don't sleep much. Anyhow,
how can I sleep with so much grief? 1170

CELIA: Surely her love will not allow
that!

LUCINDO:	¿De que las tenga te espantas?	
CELIA:	Quisiera, para un presente	
	que traigo, hallarte acostado;	
	y este viejo impertinente	1175
	tan tarde se ha levantado,	
	como va ni ve ni siente,	
	que a mediodía he venido.	
ESCUDERO:	Siempre me culpas a mí	
	de tu descuido y olvido.	1180
LUCINDO:	¿Qué traes, mi Celia, aquí?	
CELIA:	Seis camisas he traído.	
	Mira, ¡qué flamenca holanda!	
	Pues no pienses que esto es randa;	
	todo es fina cadeneta	1185
	de la aguja más perfeta	
	y de la mano más blanda.	
LUCINDO:	De la limpieza lo arguyo.	
CELIA:	Éste es corazón.	
LUCINDO:	Y ¿cuyo?	
CELIA:	De quien te le tiene dado;	1190
	que más puntas que ha labrado,	
	le quedan pasando el suyo.	
	Mandóme que te vistiese	
	la mejor, y te dijese	
	que ¡ojalá que ella pudiera	1195
	servirte de camarera!	
	Y que un abrazo te diese.	
LUCINDO:	Ése te daré yo agora,	
	y a aquella tan gran señora	
	iré a llevarle después	1200
	mil besos, para los pies	
	de donde nace la aurora.	
	Trae, Tristán, esa pieza	
	de tela, que Celia lleva	
	a su celestial belleza;	1205
	que es encarnada, y su nieve	
	tendrá mayor sutileza.	
TRISTÁN:	Ya voy.	
CELIA:	Detente, Tristán,	
	que sé que me matarán	
	si la llevo.	
LUCINDO:	¡Cosa extraña!	1210
	Mucho Fenisa se engaña,	

LUCINDO:	Is it so beyond belief?	
CELIA:	The present that I brought for you	
	makes me wish you were still in bed.	
	But there was nothing I could do	1175
	to wake this one up: he was dead	
	to everything, until I led	
	him by the hand; and now it's noon!	
SQUIRE:	You fault me if we come too soon,	
	even when the fault's yours, not mine.	1180
LUCINDO:	Let's see what makes you sing that tune,	
	Celia.	
CELIA:	Six new shirts; look how fine	
	they are; Holland cloth, every one!	
	This work is not easily done.	
	The chain stitching's done perfectly,	1185
	look how small. Not one mistake, none.	
	This hand's the finest that you'll see.	
LUCINDO:	I have never seen work so clean.	
CELIA:	There's heart in this.	
LUCINDO:	Yes, but whose heart?	
CELIA:	One who has loved you from the start;	1190
	and together the stitches mean	
	the sorrows that her heart has seen.	
	She told me to ask you to wear	
	the most elegant shirt, and tell	
	you that she wants to serve you well,	1195
	God willing; she knows how to care.	
	This embrace she asked me to share.	
LUCINDO:	How about this for an embrace!	
	I will go to her house to greet	
	your great lady, so full of grace,	1200
	and then I'll kneel and kiss her feet	
	at precious Aurora's birthplace.	
	Now, Tristan, go bring me that length	
	of new cloth, so Celia can take	
	it to heaven. Red cloth will make	1205
	her pure snowy whiteness take strength:	
	its redness paling for her sake.	
TRISTAN:	I'll get it for you.	
CELIA:	Tristan, wait;	
	if I take it home to her she	
	will kill me.	
LUCINDO:	Well, it seems to me	1210
	Fenisa hasn't got it straight:	

	si señal se puede ver	1250
	de haber dormido mujer.	
Lucindo:	¿Celos?	
Celia:	Tienes mala fama.	
	También para que mirase	
	las sábanas y almohadas,	
	porque de allá te enviase	1255
	unas de aljófar labradas.	
Lucindo:	¡Grande amor!	
Celia:	Por celos pase;	
	que está ya que es compasión	
	con tanta cara la triste.	
Lucindo:	Conozco mi obligación.	1260
	Adiós.	
Celia:	Adiós.	
Tristán:	Tú naciste	
	de pies.	
Lucindo:	Mis venturas son.	

[*Vanse.*]
[*Patio en casa de Fenisa*]
Albano y Camilio

Camilo:	¿De qué os hacéis tantas cruces?	
Albano:	¿No me tengo de espantar?	
	¿A qué más pueden llegar	1265
	unos bríos andaluces?	
Camilo:	Luego, ¿dais en que es mujer?	
Albano:	Si no es mujer, estoy loco.	
Camilo:	No será mucho.	
Albano:	No es poco,	
	si ya no hay más que perder.	1270
Camilo:	Vos ¿no veis que es desatino	
	ver un mancebo y decir	
	que es mujer?	
Albano:	¿Quién puede ver*	
	la fuerza de su destino?	
	En la más bella ciudad	1275
	que mira el sol en Europa,	
	pues todo el oro que cría	
	es para hacerle corona;	

---

*The rhyme of this verse is faulty.

	I should look to see if a trace	1250
	of some woman was any place.	
LUCINDO:	Jealousy?	
CELIA:	It's the life you led.	
	She also said to scrutinize	
	both the sheets and the pillow cases.	
	She'll send you some, just the right size,	1255
	embroidered with pearls and fine laces.	
LUCINDO:	Such love!	
CELIA:	Jealousy, to my eyes;	
	she's in such a state now, you'd fall	
	sick just looking at her so torn.	
LUCINDO:	Then I can hear my duty call.	1260
	Goodbye.	
CELIA:	Goodbye, then.	
TRISTAN:	You were born	
	on your feet.	
LUCINDO:	It's my luck, that's all.	

[They exit.]
[A courtyard at Fenisa's house]
Albano and Camilo

CAMILO:	Why do you cross yourself that way?	
ALBANO:	Why shouldn't I be so upset?	
	This Andalusian swagger gets	1265
	under my skin; that's all I say.	
CAMILO:	You think we're dealing with a woman?	
ALBANO:	If she's not a woman, I'm mad.	
CAMILO:	That might be good.	
ALBANO:	I say it's bad;	
	all this should be suffered by no man.	1270
CAMILO:	Why is it that you cannot see	
	it's mad to see a boy and label	
	him a girl?	
ALBANO:	Which of us is able	
	to see what guides his destiny?	
	In the city where the splendor	1275
	of the sun has less renown,	
	since all of Europe's gold goes there	
	to make for her a crown;	

en la gran puerta de España,
pues abriéndola dos flotas, 1280
entra por ella el gobierno
universal para todas;
en Sevilla, y en la calle
Baños de la Reina Mora,
nació Dinarda, Camilo. 1285
Tú juzgarás si es hermosa;
que yo desde que la vi
juzgaba que della sola
hiciera Zéuxis de Elena
la estampa maravillosa. 1290
Servíla, y después de un año
de paseos y de rondas,
papeles y diligencias
de terceras cautelosas,
rindióse sólo a escribirme; 1295
que si dijera otra cosa,
a mi verdad y a su sangre
haría ofensa notoria.
Todo aqueste amor fue en letras
que a letra vista se cobran; 1300
mas no se pagó ninguna,
aunque se aceptaron todas.
No hay destino tan dichoso
que no corte e interrompa
el acelerado rayo 1305
de una estrella rigurosa.
Tiene el Duque de Medina
(ya entenderás que es Sidonia)
junto a su casa en Sevilla
un corredor de pelota. 1310
Como era todo en un barrio,
frecuentaba a todas horas
su juego, o viendo o jugando;
que va esta edad por la posta.
Tiene aqueste corredor, 1315
no enfrente, sino en la popa,
las armas de los Guzmanes,
y sobre el timbre y las hojas,
que con diversos penachos
cercan el escudo y orlas, 1320
al gran don Alfonso Pérez
de Guzmán, que el Bueno nombran,
sobre el muro de Tarifa,
que al moro la daga arroja
para que mate a su hijo 1325
(¡divina hazaña española!),
y debajo de las armas
aquella sierpe espantosa

           in the finest port of Spain,
        by two great fleets made sure,   1280
           where every nations' keels,
        are universally secure;
           in the city of Seville,
        in the street of the Moorish Queen
           is where Dinarda was born,   1285
        the fairest girl you've ever seen.
           From the first time that I saw her
        I can say that she alone
           was the model for fair Helen
        carved in paint or drawn in stone.   1290
           I courted her, and in one year
        of nightly serenades,
           of love letters, and gifts,
        and go-betweens and sly charades,
           at last gave in to me, and said   1295
        she'd write to me. (If I
           said else I'd hurt her honor,
        and my own I would deny.)
           All this love poured out in love notes
        payable upon demand;   1300
           and yet none of them were cashed in
        though they all were kept in hand.
           There's no madness so well founded
        that it will not break the course
           of a flashing bolt of lightning,   1305
        or will sap a bad star's force.
           The Duke of Medina Sidonia
        is the nub of this report.
           Near his mansion in Seville
        there's a narrow handball court.   1310
           He'd be there at any hour
        since the neighborhood was small:
           playing, watching, mostly betting,
        since at his age sport is all.
           On the wall behind this ball court,   1315
        still in the neighborhood,
           is the shield of Alfonso Pérez
        who is called Guzmán the Good.
           It is set into the wall,
        crowned with pinnacles and wreath;   1320
           it's surrounded by a garland,
        and has ivy underneath.
           On the shield he throws his dagger
        down to the besieging Moor
           to kill his child: this price he'd pay   1325
        to keep his town secure.
           And below this was the horrid snake
        that in Africa he slew;

que mató en Africa, haciendo
la hazaña de Hércules corta. 1330
Entra por la boca el asta,
sale por las duras conchas
el hierro bañado en sangre,
ciñe el escudo la cola.
Estas armas, timbre y sierpe, 1335
que aquesta pared adornan,
un día estaba mirando
grande juventud ociosa,
porque acabado un partido,
y desde una parte a otra 1340
peloteándose andaban,
por ser la tarde lluviosa.
Dio un caballero a la sierpe
un pelotazo en la boca,
y dijo: "En Africa había 1345
una contienda dudosa
sobre quién mató esta sierpe;
pero sepan desde agora
que yo la he muerto, pues hay
testigos deste pelota." 1350
Respondí, aunque era de burlas,
por la afición que me toca
a la casa de Medina:
"Cuando el moro hurtó la honra
en Africa a don Alonso, 1355
deste sierpe venenosa
la boca le mandó abrir;
faltó la lengua; mas diola
don Alonso; y así el moro
perdió el crédito y la joya." 1360
"Miraré yo si la tiene,"
me replicó. Yo, la cólera
revuelta, asíle del brazo
y dije: "Lo dicho sobra;
que el Guzmán que tiene allí 1365
la daga, si hurtáis su gloria,
os la tirará a los pechos."
¡Mira qué ocasión tan loca!
Era su mayor amigo
un hermano de la diosa 1370
que idolatraban mis ojos,
pues fui de los suyos Troya.
Llegó, y dijo: "Si esta sierpe
saliera echando ponzoña
de donde la veis pintada, 1375
alguno que aquí blasona
huyera, mientras mi primo
la despedazaba, y rota,

    the deed of Hercules Guzmán
repeated here anew.   1330
     He thrust his spear into its mouth
until the scaled sides yield
    and it emerges dripping blood.
The snake's tail frames the shield.
    These arms and shield and snake   1335
that I have said this wall enjoys,
    one afternoon were gazed at
by a crowd of idle boys.
    Now, their game just ended,
they batted the ball around   1340
    without a special purpose;
a light rain was coming down.
    One young man banged the ball
into the stone mouth of the snake
    and said: "You know, an argument   1345
in Africa you still can make
    about who killed this serpent.
Well, for my part, I can say
    in front of all these witnesses
that I shot it today."   1350
    Though it was just a jest I had
to save the Duke's good name:
    "When the Moor employed this serpent
Don Alonso to defame,
    he bade the snake to bite him   1355
but the serpent had no tongue;
    and the Moor lost face and credit
when Alonso gave him one."
    "The hell he did!" the boy replied.
I grabbed him with both hands,   1360
    and trembling with anger
I exclaimed: "What I said, stands.
    Guzmán up on that shield still has
his dagger; take away
    his glory at your peril."   1365
What a crazy thing to say!
    The best friend of the brother
of my lover was this boy.
    (And although my eyes adored her,
in her own eyes I was Troy.)   1370
    The brother said: "If this snake were
to suddenly appear
    on the ground, not on the wall,
then someone who's strutting here
    would run away, while my good friend   1375
would stay and set upon
    the snake, and kill it on his shield,
just like the great Guzmán."

             honrara también sus armas
             como al Guzmán de Sidonia." 1380
             Respondí, sin reparar
             en amor ni en otra cosa:
             "Pues veamos quién la mata,
             quién huye o quién se alborota;
             que yo quiero ser la sierpe 1385
             de Guzmán, aunque Mendoza."
             Dije, y alzando la pala,
             antes de sacar la hoja,
             le di con ella en los pechos;
             y como si la persona 1390
             del propio Guzmán saliera
             a la defensa forzosa,
             despejan el corredor,
             donde tras esta deshonra
             salieron heridos tres, 1395
             y yo con justa victoria.
             Mis padres, deudos y amigos,
             por excusar la discordia
             que ya en todos engendraba,
             por discreto acuerdo toman 1400
             que me pasase a Sicilia,
             y por cartas me acomodan
             con el de Feria, virrey
             de aquestas islas famosas,
             donde la ausencia y el tiempo, 1405
             que cuanto quieren transforman,
             mudándome de Dinarda,
             de Fenisa me enamoran,
             en cuya casa hoy he visto
             este español, esta sombra, 1410
             que si no es ella, una estampa
             las hizo. Ésta fue mi historia.

CAMILO: Oid, que salen los dos.
             No paséis más adelante.

Fenisa, Dinarda, Bernardo y Fabio

FENISA:
[a Dinarda] ¿No quieres tú que me espante 1415
             de tu desdén?

DINARDA: No, ¡por Dios!
             Sino estar agradecida
             a la lealtad que he mostrado
             al Capitán.

FENISA: Tú has vengado
             muchos de quien fui homicida. 1420
             Mas mira que pensaré

	Without a thought to love	
	or any other thing, I said:	1380
	"Let's see who kills the serpent	
	and who runs away in dread;	
	I'll be the Guzmán serpent	
	though Mendoza is my name."	
	And before he could draw his sword	1385
	somehow a big stick came	
	into my hand, and I gave him	
	a good knock in the chest	
	as though I had been called to fight	
	by old Guzmán's behest.	1390
	Then the ball court poured out people	
	and dishonor both at once:	
	three good young men came out wounded—	
	every one of them a dunce.	
	My parents, servants of the Duke	1395
	and friends, to clear the air	
	of discord which now everyone	
	was feeling, sent me where	
	I would be out of sight; and so	
	they sent me for a while	1400
	to Sicily, where Feria	
	is viceroy of this isle,	
	so time and absence could transform	
	the damages; instead	
	they've turned me from Dinarda;	1405
	and instead I've lost my head	
	to Fenisa. She's my love now,	
	and I can't say that I'm sorry.	
	I saw that Spaniard in her house	
	today. I swear to glory,	1410
	he and my old love could not be	
	more alike. And that's my story.
CAMILO:	Hey, those two are coming out now.
	Don't tell me any more just yet.

Fenisa, Dinarda, Bernardo and Fabio

FENISA:
[to Dinarda]   Don't you want me to be upset   1415
              by your dishonor?

DINARDA: I don't, I vow.
              Rather I want you to be filled
              with thankfulness at my unshaken
              loyalty.

FENISA: What vengeance you've taken
              for all those others that I killed.   1420
                 But what if I tell you it's fear,

que es miedo, y que no es lealtad.

DINARDA: Sabe amor que esto es verdad.
Con él en tu casa entré;
  él me trujo, él te ha servido. 1425
¿No ves tú que no es razón
que haga tan vil traición
a un hombre tan bien nacido?
  Si solo y por mí te viera,
¡ay, Dios, cuán bien me empleara! 1430
¡Qué de veces te abrazara!
¡Qué de amores te dijera!
  Mi ventura no lo quiso,
sino que en este accidente
fuesen tus ojos la fuente, 1435
y yo su loco Narciso.
  Tántalo soy; ya me toca
el morir y enloquecer,
pues no te puedo beber,
teniendo el agua a la boca. 1440

FENISA: Bien puedes tú con secreto
ser dueño de quien te adora.

DINARDA: No me lo mandes, señora;
que soy noble te prometo.
  Osorio me trujo aquí; 1445
débole amor y dinero.

FENISA: Pagarte esas deudas quiero.

[Hablan bajo.]

CAMILO: ¿Es ella, en efeto?

ALBANO: Sí.

CAMILO: Pues ¿cómo tratan de amor
dos mujeres? ¡Loco estáis! 1450
Mas ¿por qué no os informáis
destos dos pajes mejor?

ALBANO: Aguardad, por vida mía.
¡Ah, hidalgo!

FABIO: ¿Decite a me?

ALBANO: A vos digo, si podré 1455
hablaros en cortesía.

FABIO: Di grazia, patron; ¿che cosa
mi volete?

ALBANO:
[aparte]   Estoy sin seso.

FABIO: Parlate, signore, adesso.

	not loyalty, that's moving you?	
DINARDA:	I swear by my love this is true.	
	For after all, he brought me here,	
	he opened your door, and he serves	1425
	you well. You see it would not be	
	right to commit a treachery	
	that no such well-born man deserves.	
	If only I'd first seen you when	
	I was alone, I'd love you well.	1430
	What love poems my tongue would tell!	
	My God, I would embrace you then!	
	My bad luck precluded those kisses.	
	But now fate has played us for fools,	
	for your eyes are like crystal pools,	1435
	and I am your insane Narcissus.	
	I'm Tantalus, of whom it's sung	
	he could not die for going mad:	
	I cannot drink you, though I've had	
	the cool liquid here on my tongue.	1440
FENISA:	Surely you know that secretly	
	you can possess one who loves you.	
DINARDA:	My lady, please don't make me do	
	that, it wounds my nobility.	
	Osorio brought me, I confess.	1445
	I owe him love; and money, too.	
FENISA:	I will repay those debts for you.	

[They speak quietly.]

CAMILO:	Is she the woman you mean?	
ALBANO:	Yes.	
CAMILO:	How can those two women be wooing	
	each other? You must be insane.	1450
	If you're going on in that vein,	
	see what those two pages are doing.	
ALBANO:	Hey, wait a moment, my good man:	
	what's going on?	
FABIO:	Do you mean me?	
ALBANO:	I do. Do me the courtesy	1455
	of answering me, if you can.	
FABIO:	*Di grazzia, patron*; please forgive.	
	Che cosa?	
ALBANO:		
[aside]	I can't believe this.	
FABIO:	Speak, speak, *signore*, I insist.	

ALBANO: *[aparte]*	¡Ay, bella Dinarda hermosa! ¿Quién es este caballero?	1460
FABIO:	¿Questo gentiluomo?	
ALBANO:	Sí.	
FABIO:	Il signor Ruggiero.	
ALBANO:	¡Ah! ¿Sí? ¿Su nombre propio es Rugero? Pues, ¿de dónde es?	
FABIO:	Veneziano, benchè venuto di Roma.	1465
ALBANO:	¿No es español?	
CAMILO: *[aparte]*	¡Qué ira toma!	
FABIO:	¡Guarda! ¿Spagnuolo marrano? ¡Cancaro che venga a tutti li traditori spagnuoli, furfanti, ladri, mariuoli, asassini per tre scuti!	1470
ALBANO:	Camilo, ¡cosa inhumana! ¡Por Dios, que me vuelve loco!	
FABIO:	Aspetta di grazia un poco, la canzone siciliana: Se tutta la Sicilia fosse macarrone, il faro di Messina vino moscatello, il monte Mongibello formaggio grattato, e tutto lo spagnuolo fossino ammazzato, ¡como trionfaria lo siciliano!	1475 1480 1485

ALBANO:
[aside] (Oh, Sweet Dinarda, as I live!)   1460
       Tell me, who is this noble sir?

FABIO: *Questo gentiluomo?*

ALBANO: I know.

FABIO: *Il signor Rugiero.*

ALBANO: Ah. So
      his name's Rugiero, I infer?
        Then where is he from?

FABIO: *Veneziano*   1465
    venuto di Roma.

ALBANO: He's not
      Spanish?

CAMILO:
[aside]   (How angry he has got!)

FABIO: Hey, wait! *Spagnuolo marrano?*
      Cancaro che venga a tutti
      li traditori spagnuoli,   1470
      furfanti, ladri, mariuoli,
      asassini per tre scuti!

ALBANO: I'm going crazy; something's wrong,
      Camilo. Do you think he's phony?

FABIO: *Aspetta la mia canzone.*   1475
      Listen to my Sicilian song:
        Se tutta la Sicilia
        fosse macarrone,
        il faro di Messina
        vino moscatello,   1480
        il monte Mongibello,
        formaggio grattato,
        e tutto lo spagnuolo
        fossino ammazzato,
        ¡come trionfaria   1485
        lo siciliano!

      [If all of Sicily were but
      a big bowl of spaghetti,
      a bottle of sweet wine Messina's
      lighthouse on her jetty,
      if Mongibello Mountain
      were a mound of grated cheese,
      if every single Spaniard
      could be ground to pulp with ease,
      then what happiness you'd see
      in all of Sicily.]

CAMILO:	Basta, que ya el pajecillo os da la vaya.	
ALBANO:	Aguardad; que él me dirá la verdad.	
FABIO: *[aparte a Bernardo]*	Apenas puedo sufrillo.	1490
BERNARDO:	Disimula, Fabio, un poco, no conozcan a Dinardo.	
FABIO:	Muero de risa, Bernardo. ¿Hablo bien?	
BERNARDO:	Vuélvesle loco.	
ALBANO:	Piglia este escudo, fanciullo, y dime...	1495
FABIO:	¿Che vuoi di me?	
ALBANO:	Esta, ¿es mujer?	
FABIO:	¿Come? ¿Che? ¿Volete pigliar trastullo? ¿Donna lo signore mio? ¡Oimè! ¿Che diavolo è questo?	1500
ALBANO:	Yo sé que de hombre se ha puesto.	
FABIO:	No mi fastidiar, ¡per Dio! Ne mi faccia intrar in cólera. ¡Femmina far lo signore!	
BERNARDO:	¿Femmina?	
FABIO:	Sí.	
BERNARDO:	¡Un traditore! Tace per tua vita e tóllera.	1505
CAMILO:	Necio andáis.	
ALBANO:	¿Cómo?	
CAMILO:	¡Por Dios!...	
ALBANO:	En vuestra malicia he dado.	
CAMILO:	Que pienso que han sospechado alguna fealdad de vos!	1510
ALBANO:	Pues ¿preguntar si es mujer os parece sospechoso?	
CAMILO:	Que nos vamos es forzoso.	
ALBANO:	Y forzoso enloquecer.	

CAMILO:	Enough! You know this little page is pulling your leg.	
ALBANO:	Hold on there! I'll make him tell the truth, I swear.	
FABIO: [aside to Bernardo]	Look how he puts me in a rage!	1490
BERNARDO:	Keep it up, Fabio. That's not bad. Don't let them recognize Dinardo.	
FABIO:	I'm dying of laughter, Bernardo. How'm I doing?	
BERNARDO:	He's going mad.	
ALBANO:	*Piglio este escudo* now, and tell me something...	1495
FABIO:	Eh? *Che voi di me?*	
ALBANO:	Is she a woman?	
FABIO:	*Come? Che?* Are you going insane as well? *E donna mi signore?* No! Some *diavolo*'s clouded your eyes.	1500
ALBANO:	I know her clothing's a disguise.	
FABIO:	You're making me angry, *per Dio*! Why insist on such craziness? *Femmina far lo signori!*	
BERNARDO:	*Femmina.*	
FABIO:	*Si.*	
BERNARDO:	*Un traditore!* Sir, you're causing me great distress!	1505
CAMILO:	You must be crazy.	
ALBANO:	What?	
CAMILO:	By God...	
ALBANO:	Can this be malice I detect?	
CAMILO:	I think that these people suspect you've done something ugly, or odd.	1510
ALBANO:	Is she a woman? What's so very wrong in our attempting to know?	
CAMILO:	It's necessary that we go.	
ALBANO:	Going mad is what's necessary!	

Camilo:	Hablad después a Fenisa;	1515
	que nadie os dirá mejor	
	si es hombre o mujer.	
Albano:	¡Oh amor!	

[Vanse Albano y Camilo.]

Fabio:	Muriéndome estoy de risa.	
Bernardo:	¿Fuéronse?	
Fabio:	Los dos se van.	
Bernardo:	Pues yo sé, Fabio, que quedo	1520
	con más malicia que miedo.	
Fabio:	¿Qué sospechas te la dan?	
Bernardo:	De que Dinardo es mujer.	
Fabio:	Eso me parece a mí,	
	aunque nunca me atreví	1525
	a procurallo saber;	
	fuera de que está Fenisa	
	loca por él.	
Bernardo:	Es verdad;	
	aunque la dificultad	
	con que la trata, me avisa.	1530
Fabio:	Luego el respeto que tiene	
	al Capitán, ¿es fingido?	
Bernardo:	Pienso que todo lo ha sido,	
	y que de otra causa viene.	
Fabio:	Desde hoy emprendo saber	1535
	si es mujer.	
Bernardo:	Y yo, ¡por Dios!	
Fabio:	Pues comencemos los dos	
	desde agora a pretender.	
Fenisa: *[a Dinarda]*	En fin, don Juan, ¿te resuelves	
	a no pagar este amor?	1540
Dinarda:	Conociendo mi valor,	
	Fenisa, ¿a probarme vuelves?	
	Haz una cosa: da traza	
	que este capitán se ausente,	
	pues tú podrás fácilmente	1545
	esto, o mudarle la plaza;	
	y en su ausencia te prometo	
	corresponder a tu amor.	
Fenisa:	Pues, mi bien, de tu valor	

CAMILO:	Ask Fenisa later. No one can tell man and woman apart better than she can.	1515
ALBANO:	Oh my heart!	

[Albano and Camilo exit.]

FABIO:	I can't stop laughing. I'm undone!	
BERNARDO:	Have they gone?	
FABIO:	They're both out of sight.	
BERNARDO:	For my part, Fabio, I've been made far more curious than afraid.	1520
FABIO:	Then you suspect that all's not right?	
BERNARDO:	He's a woman, haven't you guessed?	
FABIO:	Of course, why not? I am prepared to believe it; but I've not dared to put the matter to the test. In either case, one thing is sure: Fenisa loves him.	1525
BERNARDO:	I can see that from the strange difficulty with which she deals with him — or her.	1530
FABIO:	So that this great show of respect for the Captain was just pretense?	
BERNARDO:	I think that none of it makes sense. There's some other cause, I suspect.	
FABIO:	Starting today I'll try to find out if she's a woman.	1535
BERNARDO:	Me too.	
FABIO:	Then we're resolved: let's go and do it now, since we are of one mind.	
FENISA: *[to Dinarda]*	Don Juan, then do you mean to say you don't love me as I love you?	1540
DINARDA:	You know me Fenisa, why do you keep pushing at me this way? Do one thing: find some scheme to make the Captain go away; you can do that for me; make that your plan, deny him your house, for my sake. And when he's gone I promise you I will love you as you love me.	1545
FENISA:	I believe your sincerity,	

                    fío, y la palabra aceto.   1550

Celia

CELIA: Aquí está Lucindo.

FENISA: ¿Quién?

CELIA: El mercader de Valencia.

FENISA: Dame, mis ojos, licencia.

DINARDA: Licencia tienes, mi bien.

[Vanse Fenisa y Celia.]
Bernardo y Fabio, retirados

DINARDA: Siguiendo un loco pensamiento vine   1555
                    desde Sevilla hasta Sicilia, cielos:
                    de vergüenza y honor rompí los velos;
                    que no hay cosa que amor no desatine.
                        Mas ¿qué le sirve al alma que camine
                    entre tantas congojas y desvelos,   1560
                    si sacándome amor, me vuelven celos,
                    y no sé de los dos a cuál me incline?
                        Aquí le hallé, con nuevo pensamiento
                    el alma, el gusto en otro amor extraño,
                    con que mudó mi desatino intento.   1565
                        No más perjura fe, no más engaño;
                    que es para heridas de un amor violento
                    divina contrayerba el desengaño.

Lucindo y Tristán

LUCINDO: ¿No le dio Celia mi recaudo?

TRISTÁN: Pienso
                    que tiene algunos huéspedes Fenisa.   1570

LUCINDO: ¿Es caballo de Troya aquesta casa,
                    que siempre está preñada de armas y hombres?

TRISTÁN: Pues ¿cuál audiencia pública, Lucindo,
                    iguala al patio de una cortesana?
                    Aquí tiene sus horas, y aquí juzga.   1575
                    Verás los abogados y terceros,
                    los solicitadores y escribanos,
                    que le envían papeles de procesos,
                    sobornos de regalos y presentes,
                    pleitos en vista, pleitos en revista.   1580
                    A unos despacha y a otros entretiene,
                    como tienen favor o traen dineros.

LUCINDO: ¿Quién es este español que tan solícito
                    frecuenta aquesta casa?

| | and what you ask of me I'll do. | 1550 |

[Celia and the above]

CELIA:	Here is Lucindo.
FENISA:	Who?
CELIA:	The one with the Valencian commission.
FENISA:	My love, please give me your permission.
DINARDA:	Permission? Consider it done.

[Celia and Fenisa exit.]
Dinarda; Fabio and Bernardo to one side

DINARDA:	With my demented thoughts leading the way	1555
	I left Seville and came to Sicily;	
	I tore off honor's veil, and modesty,	
	for there is nothing love can't turn astray.	
	And yet, what gains my soul from this display	
	of courage, since my road is lunacy;	1560
	if what begins as love, to jealousy	
	soon turns, and I can't choose which to obey?	
	I found him here, but found his soul had turned	
	to take its pleasures from another heart.	
	To quit this foolish quest is my intent.	1565
	No more deceit, no more love unreturned;	
	the antidote for love's infecting dart	
	lies in sweet holy disillusionment.	

Lucindo Tristan, and the above

LUCINDO:	Did Celia tell you what I said?	
TRISTAN:	I think Fenisa's entertaining several guests.	1570
LUCINDO:	Has her house now become a Trojan horse, its belly overstuffed with men and arms?	
TRISTAN:	Lucindo, have you ever seen a court as crowded as a courtesan's courtyard?	
	Her office hours are here, she judges here.	1575
	It's full of lawyers, clerks, and go-betweens, of prosecutors, notaries and scribes who bring her briefs that summarize each case, and gifts and favors they intend as bribes	
	to take their brand new cases and appeals.	1580
	Some she dispatches, some she entertains, according to their power, and their purse.	
LUCINDO:	Who is this Spaniard, so solicitous, who hangs around her house?	

TRISTÁN: Este es.... Sospecho
que es del alma.

LUCINDO: Y yo ¿qué soy?

TRISTÁN: Del cuerpo.   1585

LUCINDO: Donaire tienes. Si Fenisa vive
en el cuidado que la ves conmigo,
si le cuesto regalos y dineros,
¿cuál otro puede haber que sea del alma?

TRISTÁN: ¡Qué chapetón estás en estas Indias!   1590
¿No sabes tú que hay almas en que caben
más de dos y de tres y de trescientos?
Cuando ves escribir treinta papeles
una buena señora a treinta amantes,
cuando ves que otros tantos la visitan,   1595
cuando ves que a uno pide el coche, a otro
la basquiña, a cual tiene dentro en casa,
a cual habla en la reja, a cual de noche,
¿has de pensar que es alma edificada
a la traza de un grande monasterio   1600
en que hay su dormitorio con sus celdas,
que de una puerta adentro caben todas?

LUCINDO:
[a Dinarda]   Hablaros, caballero, he deseado.

DINARDA: No menos yo, que os soy aficionado.
Mas si es de celos de Fenisa, os pido   1605
no los tengáis de mí, porque a su casa
me ha traído cuidado diferente.
¿Cuándo os volvéis a España?

LUCINDO: Yo he pensado
que por todo este mes, porque a mi gusto
he despachado cuanto della truje.   1610
Mas tiéneme cautivo el desta dama.

DINARDA: Con vos me pienso ir hasta Valencia,
aunque soy de Sevilla; porque quiero
ir a la corte y pretender en ella
la remuneración de mis servicios   1615
primero que a mi patria vuelva.

BERNARDO:
[a Tristán]   Diga,
señor lacayo, ¿es español acaso?

TRISTÁN: Y ellos, ¿qué son, señores pajarotes?

FABIO: Noi altri siamo certi gentiluomini,
venuti adesso adesso di Venezia.   1620
Dica di grazia, e non montar in collera,

TRISTAN: He's...I suspect
he has her soul.

LUCINDO: And I?

TRISTAN: You have her body.

LUCINDO: You're making fun of me. If she is so
circumspect in the way she deals with me,
and if she showers me with gifts and cash,
how can you say some other has her soul?

TRISTAN: You sound like you have just stepped off the boat.
Aren't you aware that some souls are so big
that two, three or three hundred fit inside?
When you see some good lady writing notes
of love to thirty lovers at one time,
and then see thirty lovers paying call;
when you see her ask one to pay her coach,
and one her house accounts, and when you see
one in her house, one at her window grille,
you must conclude her soul's an edifice
like some great monastery, tall and wide,
whose dormitory halls are lined with cells,
one outside door but many doors within.

LUCINDO:
[to Dinarda] Good sir, you know I'd like to speak with you.

DINARDA: No less than I, who hold you in esteem.
If you're jealous of Fenisa, I beg
you not to be of me, because I came
here to her house because of something else.
When are you going back to Spain?

LUCINDO: I thought
I'd stay throughout the month, because I've done
my business and enjoyed myself as well.
Besides, I have become this lady's slave.

DINARDA: Although I'm from Seville, I'd like to sail
to Valencia with you, because I want
to go to court and ask remuneration
for what I have accomplished here, before
I go back home again.

BERNARDO:
[to Tristan] Sir Lackey, please
explain to me, is your master from Spain?

TRISTAN: And yours, is he some kind of noble bird?

FABIO: *Noi altri siamo certi gentiluomini,*
venutti adesso adesso di Venezia.
Dica di grazia, e non montar in collera,

	come si chiama in Spagna quella lira con che fanno ai caballi chiquichiqui.	
Tristán:	Llámase el diablo que te lleve.	
Bernardo:	¿Deso no más se corre un hombre tan discreto?	1625
Tristán:	¿No saben qué han de hacer, señores pajes? Tener respeto a un hombre de mi término.	
Fabio:	Sopra la mia parola, siate sano.	
Tristán:	No entiendo de parola; háganse afuera; que les daré en mi lengua cuatro coces.	1630
Fabio:	Bene dice, ¡per Dio! la è una bestia.	
Lucindo: [a Dinarda]	Pues tendré a gran merced que nos hablemos.	
Dinarda:	Adonde digo estoy.	
Lucindo:	Iré a buscaros.	
Bernardo:	Fabio, don Juan se va.	
Fabio:	Señor lacayo, a rivederci a l'altro mondo.	
Tristán:	¡Pícaro! Caballero soy yo.	1635
Fabio:	Mi racommando.	
Dinarda:	Pajes...	
Bernardo:	Señor...	
Dinarda:	Hacia Palacio vamos.	
Bernardo: [aparte a Dinarda]	¿Qué hay de Fenisa?	
Dinarda:	Amores y promesas.	
Fabio:	¿No te da nada?	
Dinarda:	Ya se va trazando.	
Bernardo: [aparte a Fabio]	¿Parécete mujer?	
Fabio:	Probarlo puedo; mas es probar cuchillo con el dedo.	1640

[Vanse Dinarda, Bernardo y Fabio.]
Celia

| Celia: | Mi señora te suplica,
Lucindo, que la perdones; |

	—how do you say in Spanish?—*quella lira*
	con che fanno ai caballi chiquichiqui?
TRISTAN:	Call him the Devil, Devil take you.
BERNARDO:	Why

TRISTAN: Call him the Devil, Devil take you.

BERNARDO: Why
get so upset at something small as that?   1625

TRISTAN: Why don't you pages know how to behave?
You must show more respect to one like me.

FABIO: *Sopra la mia parola, siate sano.*

TRISTAN: Drop that parola stuff. You'd best take care
or I'll tell you what for in my own tongue.   1630

FABIO: *Bene dice, per Dio!, la è una bestia.*

LUCINDO:
[to Dinarda]   I'd consider it a favor if we talked.

DINARDA: You'll find me where I said.

LUCINDO: I'll come for you.

BERNARDO: Fabio, Don Juan is going.

FABIO: Sir Lackey,
a rivederci a l'altro mondo.

TRISTAN: Knave,   1635
I am a gentleman.

FABIO: *Mi racommando.*

DINARDA: Pages.

BERNARDO: My lord.

DINARDA: Let's to the palace now.

BERNARDO:
[to Dinarda]   What's with Fenisa?

DINARDA: Love and promises.

FABIO: Did she give you something?

DINARDA: It's in the works.

BERNARDO:
[aside to Fabio] Is she a girl?

FABIO: I'll put it to the test,   1640
like testing knives for sharpness with your thumb.

[*Dinarda, Bernardo and Fabio exit.*]

CELIA: Lucindo, my lady prefers
that you grant her pardon just now;

	que por ciertas ocasiones	
	que aquí no te significa,	1645
	no puede salir a verte.	
Lucindo:	Ya, Celia, me dio a entender	
	que no es posible querer	
	la mujer que se divierte.	
	Está muy entretenida;	1650
	es lindo don Juan de Lara.	
	Habrá picado en la cara:	
	ahí, Celia, estará perdida.	
	Conozco su condición:	1655
	toda mujer que profesa	
	esta cólera francesa,	
	no es firme de corazón.	
	¡Bueno quedaré yo agora,	
	que su amor loco en exceso	
	me ha puesto!	
Celia:	No digas eso,	1660
	Lucindo, de mi señora;	
	que eres la vida por quien	
	recibe aliento vital,	
	y aunque el verte le esté mal,	
	ella lo dirá más bien.	1665

[Vase.]

Lucindo:	Escucha.
Tristán:	Enojada fue.
Lucindo:	¿Qué le dije?
Tristán:	Ha sido error llamar fingido su amor.

[Éntranse Lucindo y Tristán tras Celia.]
[Sala en casa de Fenisa]
Lucindo y Tristán

Lucindo: *[viendo salir a Fenisa]*	¿Qué es esto, Tristán?	
Tristán:	No sé.	

[Sale Fenisa, de luto, con una carta en la mano, y Celia sigue a su ama.]

Lucindo:	¡Luto vos, señora mía!	1670
	¿Qué toca es ésa y qué llanto?	
Fenisa:	Para no afligiros tanto,	
	no veros, mi bien, quería;	
	mas como allá dentro oí	
	ofender mi justo amor,	1675

	there are reasons which don't allow	
	her to come, through no fault of hers;	1645
	it's really none of your concern.	
LUCINDO:	Celia, I can't love anyone	
	like her who's so obsessed with fun:	
	that's one I have come to learn.	
	She's doing very well, I've thought.	1650
	Don Juan's a really handsome man.	
	He's taken beauty's bait, I can	
	see that. Celia, the man is caught!	
	I know perfectly well what's wrong:	
	a woman this fond of romance	1655
	has got to have been born in France:	
	that's where these fickle hearts belong.	
	Look what a state she's put me in!	
	This crazy loving of hers brings	
	me to the brink.	
CELIA:	Don't say such things,	1660
	Lucindo; don't even begin.	
	You are her very world, the man	
	who gives her life, puts meaning in it;	
	if she can't see you right this minute	
	she'll explain later when she can.	1665

[She exits.]

LUCINDO:	Wait.
TRISTAN:	She's angry. Look at her go.
LUCINDO:	What did I say?
TRISTAN:	A great mistake
	to say Fenisa's love was fake.

[Lucindo and Tristan go in after Celia.]
[A room in Fenisa's house]
Lucindo and Tristan

LUCINDO: *[seeing Fenisa enter]*	Now what's this, Tristan?	
TRISTAN:	I don't know.	

[Fenisa enters dressed in mourning, with a letter in her hand; Celia follows her mistress.]

LUCINDO:	In mourning clothes, my lady? How	1670
	can that be? And tears? Why such weeping?	
FENISA:	To spare you my grief, I was keeping	
	myself away from you just now.	
	But then I heard a reference	
	to false love, and I could not let	1675

estimo tanto mi honor,
que a defenderle salí.
    Vos sois la vida que vivo,
vos los ojos con que veo,
el gusto con que deseo 1680
el que de veros recibo.
    Sois el aire que alimenta
las olas del corazón,
vos sois la respiración
que para vivir me alienta. 1685
    Sois el nervimiento mío,
sois la fe de mi verdad,
la ley de mi voluntad,
el alma de mi albedrío.
    Y pues en tanto dolor 1690
os hablo tan tiernamente,
creed que no es accidente,
sino verdadero amor.

LUCINDO: Fenisa y fénix, en quien
se abrasa el alma que os di 1695
para renovarse en mí,
¿qué es lo que tenéis, mi bien?
    ¿Qué os puede haber sucedido,
dulce prenda destos ojos,
que en nubes de agua y de enojos 1700
vuestro sol tiene escondido?
    ¿Qué luto es éste que enluta
tu resplandeciente esfera?
¿Qué ocasión en ti tan fiera
su sentimiento ejecuta? 1705
    ¡Vos eclipsada, mi sol!
¿Vos con cerco de agua y llanto?
¡Que dure mi vida tanto!

FENISA: ¡Ay, mi adorado español!
    Si queja podéis tener, 1710
es que estando vos presente
me pueda ajeno accidente
afligir y entristecer.
    Mas si sabéis la ocasión,
pienso que disculparéis 1715
estas lágrimas que veis,
porque, en fin, de sangre son.

LUCINDO: ¿Cómo de sangre?

FENISA: Pues ya
todo saberlo queréis,
en esta carta veréis 1720
la causa y quien me la da.

	my honor suffer such a threat,	
	so I came out in my defense.	
	Of my life, love, you are the measure.	
	Your eyes are looking through my own.	
	Of all the pleasures that I've known,	1680
	the sight of you gives me more pleasure.	
	You are the warm wind that sustains,	
	Lucindo, my heart's beating wings;	
	you are the very air that brings	
	life to my lungs, blood to my veins.	1685
	You are the nerves with which I feel;	
	you are the faith that makes me true;	
	your strength is what makes me strong; you	
	teach my soul which things are real.	
	And since from the midst of such grief	1690
	I cry out so pitifully,	
	it is true love that speaks through me,	
	not false. This must be your belief.	
LUCINDO:	Fenisa, my Phoenix, in whom	
	the soul I placed burns with bright flame,	1695
	renewing itself in my name,	
	tell me, what is this sense of doom?	
	What has happened, sweet paragon,	
	bright love light of my loving eyes?	
	Why have such clouds of tears and sighs	1700
	marred the face of your shining sun?	
	What mourning clothes are these? What night	
	has come to your resplendent sphere?	
	What accident is so severe	
	that it's given you such a fright?	1705
	How could your sun be in eclipse?	
	I've never seen such grief and tears.	
	How can I live through such wild fears?	
FENISA:	Oh, my sweet Spaniard, my heart skips.	
	One thing your anger justifies,	1710
	and that's that while I was with you,	
	my trouble with someone else threw	
	me into such laments and sighs.	
	The real reason will give you pause,	
	my love; in spite of what appears,	1715
	there is no water in these tears:	
	they're blood, and honor is the cause.	
LUCINDO:	What do you mean, honor?	
FENISA:	You claim	
	you want to find out everything;	
	here, read this letter explaining	1720
	what it is and who is to blame.	

LUCINDO:
[lee] "Hermana mía, y la postrera vez que podré
llamaros hermana: a mí me han sentenciado
a muerte en vista y revista. La parte, por
ruegos del Príncipe de Butera, perdona por
2.000 ducados. No tengo humano remedio de
pagarlos; si allá hubiere alguno, vuestra sangre
soy, y anduve en las entrañas mismas donde
anduviste. De Mesina, etc. — Camilo Fénix."
　　¡Extraña carta!

CELIA: 　　　　　¡Ay de mí,
que se cayó desmayada!

TRISTÁN: La carta es tierna.

LUCINDO: 　　　　　¡Mi amada
Lucinda!

TRISTÁN: 　　¿No hay agua?

CELIA: 　　　　　　Sí. 　　　　1725

LUCINDO: 　Pero no vayas por ella,
que están mis ojos presentes;
que es vergüenza de otras fuentes
que de las suyas traella.
　Coge aquí, Celia, aunque tanto 　　1730
dolor tiene el pecho lleno,
que podrá darle veneno
una dracma de mi llanto.
　¡Ah mi bien! ¿Vivís? Mas ¿quién
preguntara tal error? 　　　　1735
Vivir yo es señal mayor,
porque vos viváis también.
　Volved en vos, que habrá medio
para ese mal.

FENISA: 　　　　　¡Ay, mi hermano!

LUCINDO: ¿Habla?

TRISTÁN: 　　　Sí.

LUCINDO: 　　　　Amor soberano 　　1740
de tu piedad fue remedio.
　León fue mi sentimiento,
que la muerta gloria mía
volvió a la vida, que había
llegado al último aliento. 　　　1745
　¿Qué puedo yo hacer por vos
y ese desdichado hermano?

FENISA: Todo remedio es en vano.

LUCINDO: Busquémoselo los dos.

LUCINDO:
[reads] "My sister, for the last time that I can call you sister, they have sentenced me to death, signed and sealed. The injured party, at the insistence of the Prince of Butera, will forgive me for two thousand ducats. There is no human way I can pay them. If someone there can manage it, I am your flesh and blood, for I shared the womb with you. From Messina etc. Camilo Fenix."
    What a strange letter.

CELIA: Look at this: She's fainted dead away, I fear.

TRISTAN: What a tragic letter.

LUCINDO: My dear love.

TRISTAN: Is there water?

CELIA: Yes, there is. 1725

LUCINDO: You don't have to go bring her some.
My two eyes can be the supply.
It would be wrong, the way I cry,
that from another source it come.
    Here, Celia, gather up these streams. 1730
Though such sharp torments my chest fill
that I fear they will do her ill.
For such tears are poison, it seems.
    Ah, my love! Are you alive? Yet
what a foolish question. If I 1735
still live I know you did not die,
for your life holds my life in debt.
    Wake up. I'm sure we can attack
this in some way.

FENISA: Oh. Oh, my brother...

LUCINDO: Did she speak?

TRISTAN: Yes, she did.

LUCINDO: Another 1740
miracle of love's brought her back.
    As she was drawing her last breath
the lion strength of my love for
my dearest opened up life's door
and drew Fenisa back from death. 1745
    Tell me what I can do for you,
and for that poor brother of yours.

FENISA: For my problems there are no cures.

LUCINDO: We can find one between us two.

FENISA:	El que en esto puede haber	1750
	es que, pues habéis vendido	
	la hacienda que habéis traído,	
	según dijisteis ayer,	
	sobre mis joyas y hacienda	
	me prestéis dos mil ducados;	1755
	que estos rigores pasados...	
LUCINDO:	No tratéis, mi bien, de prenda;	
	que no es pequeño el amor	
	y obligación que yo os debo.	
FENISA:	Herrarme queréis de nuevo,	1760
	tenéis español valor.	
LUCINDO:	Pero advertid, gloria mía,	
	que un mercader sin dinero	
	es como amor sin tercero,	
	es como sin luz el día.	1765
	Habéisme de prometer	
	pagar en breve; que ya	
	mi partida cerca está,	
	y será echarme a perder...	
FENISA:	Luego que salga mi hermano,	1770
	unas casas venderemos	
	que cerca de aquí tenemos,	
	y os pagaré de mi mano.	
	Pero tomad, por mi vida,	
	mis joyas: yo gusto desto.	1775
LUCINDO:	Tristán, parte a casa presto,	
	y en el arca guarnecida	
	un gato hallarás, que tiene	
	en oro dos mil ducados.	
	Esta es la llave.	
CELIA:	¡Qué honrados	1780
	pensamientos!	
FENISA:	Al fin viene	
	de tierra, ejemplo en el mundo	
	en hacer bien y amistad.	
LUCINDO:	Más debo a tu voluntad.	
FENISA:	Débesme un amor profundo.	1785
LUCINDO:	¿No vas, Tristán?	
TRISTÁN:	Sí, señor.	
LUCINDO:	Pues, ¿qué miras?	
TRISTÁN: *[aparte a su amo]*	¿Estás loco?	

FENISA:	The only one I can think of	1750
	is that having already sold	
	all of the goods you brought for gold,	
	as you said yesterday, my love,	
	is that you make a loan to me	
	against all my jewels and goods	1755
	of two thousand ducats; I could...	
LUCINDO:	Let's not talk of security.	
	That I'm in debt to you is plain,	
	both for love, and for what I owe.	
FENISA:	You'd brand me again! How you show	1760
	the spirit of a man of Spain!	
LUCINDO:	Just don't forget, my love's delight,	
	a businessman of cash stripped clean's	
	like love without a go-between,	
	or like a day without daylight.	1765
	You must swear to repay the debt	
	right away, for I have to go	
	away from here soon, and I know	
	my life is lost if I don't get...	
FENISA:	As soon as my brother is free	1770
	we'll sell some houses that we own	
	near here; then I'll repay the loan	
	from my own hand; have faith in me.	
	But still, I want you to hold my	
	jewels. Please, honor my request.	1775
LUCINDO:	Tristan, you remember the chest	
	we left home in our lodgings? I	
	want you to go there and collect	
	all the gold; the strongbox is full.	
	Take this key.	
CELIA:	What honorable	1780
	sentiments!	
FENISA:	What do you expect	
	from one who came here from the place	
	known for friendship and noble deeds?	
LUCINDO:	Your love my own poor love exceeds.	
FENISA:	Your love is strong as this embrace.	1785
LUCINDO:	You can go, Tristan.	
TRISTAN:	Yes, my lord.	
LUCINDO:	Speak up, I say.	
TRISTAN: [aside to Lucindo]	Are you deranged?	

LUCINDO:	Déjame ser noble un poco,	
	y no ingrato a tanto amor;	
	yo conozco esta mujer,	1790
	y yo lo sabré cobrar.	
TRISTÁN:	Las joyas puedes tomar.	
LUCINDO:	Cuando fuere menester.	
FENISA:	¿Qué os dice Tristán?	
LUCINDO:	Querría	
	que vuestras joyas tomara;	1795
	es mercader, y repara	
	en prendas.	
FENISA:	¡Por vida mía!....	

[Vase Tristán.]

LUCINDO:	Por vida vuestra, mi bien,	
	que basta un cabello en prenda	
	de más oro, y nadie entienda	1800
	que otra quiero que me den.	
	Las almas, ¿tienen valor?	
FENISA:	¿Qué mayor?	
LUCINDO:	Si se celebra	
	que de cada sutil hebra	
	cuelga mil almas amor,	1805
	¿qué más prenda que un cabello	
	donde mil almas están?	
	Mas voy a ver si Tristán	
	yerra o acierta con ello,	
	para que lo traiga al punto.	1810
FENISA:	Vente hoy a comer conmigo,	
	bizarro español.	
LUCINDO:	Yo digo	
	que vendré.	
FENISA:	Y contigo junto	
	vendrá todo el bien que tengo.	
	Ven, mi señor, y encamina	1815
	este dinero a Mesina.	
LUCINDO:	Espérame, que ya vengo.	

[Vase.]

FENISA:	¿Fuése?	
CELIA:	La escalera abajo.	
FENISA:	Mamóla su señoría.	
CELIA:	Mientras vemos luz es día:	1820

LUCINDO:	Let me be noble for a change, and give this love its just reward. Anyway, I know how to read. this woman; I'll collect the debt.	1790
TRISTAN:	Take the jewels to hedge the bet.	
LUCINDO:	I'll do that later if there's need.	
FENISA:	What's that, Tristan?	
LUCINDO:	He'd have me take your jewels for security. He's a merchant, who likes to see something in hand.	1795
FENISA:	For pity's sake!	

[Tristan exits.]

LUCINDO:	No pity, my love. Just one hair from your golden ringlets stands bond for all of my treasure. Beyond that I need nothing else, I swear. Who can put a price on a soul?	1800
FENISA:	No one.	
LUCINDO:	Because we realize that every single hair's a prize which a thousand hearts unroll. If that is so, what bond could be stronger than a lock of your hair? To make sure Tristan doesn't err and bring the wrong box, I'll go see he gets it right. Farewell, my love.	1805 1810
FENISA:	Come have lunch with me today, you wonderful Spaniard.	
LUCINDO:	I will do it.	
FENISA:	Love, you are the essence of all the good in my life today. Hurry back with the money so that to Messina it can go.	1815
LUCINDO:	Wait, I will be back right away.	

[He exits.]

FENISA:	Is he gone?	
CELIA:	He went down the stairs.	
FENISA:	His lordship gobbled up the bait.	
CELIA:	It's still daylight; don't celebrate	1820

	no hagas fiestas y habla bajo;	
	que se puede arrepentir	
	de aquí a la posada el hombre;	
	mas, ¿a quién hay que no asombre	
	tu artificioso vivir?	1825
FENISA:	Calla, que es cosa de risa;	
	como eso pescar verás.	
	No se ha de olvidar jamás	
	del *Anzuelo de Fenisa*.	
	Quedo, que llaman.	
CELIA:	¿Quién sube?	1830
FENISA:	Mira si maulla aquel gato.	

Tristán

TRISTÁN:	Para no mostrarme ingrato,	
	ni un instante me detuve;	
	aquí viene aquel dinero.	
FENISA:	Muestra, a ver; escudos son;	1835
	Tristán, pilla este doblón,	
	y dile a aquel caballero	
	que venga luego a comer;	
	que le aguardo agradecida,	
	y vuélvete, por mi vida,	1840
	que tengo un poco que hacer.	
TRISTÁN: *[aparte]*	De lo prestado barato...	
	¡Oh, qué mal indicio es!	
	Este ratón al revés	
	nos ha cogido este gato.	1845

[Vase.]

FENISA:	¿Bajóse?	
CELIA:	Iba murmurando.	
FENISA:	También murmuran los ríos,	
	y de oir y ver sus bríos	
	se están los peces holgando.	
	¿Será gran descompostura	1850
	besar este gato?	
CELIA:	No.	
	que es de algalia, y pienso yo	
	que de su aliento asegura.	
FENISA:	Ves aquí, Celia, a Lucindo	
	besado en forma de gato.	1855
CELIA:	¿No hay mujer que sin recato	
	quiere y besa a un perro lindo?	

	just yet. Speak low; don't put on airs;	
	for that good man can still repent	
	in between your lodgings and his.	
	Who can witness your artifice	
	and not feel great astonishment?	1825

FENISA: Hush. It's hardly anything. Look
at me, if you'd learn how to fish.
No finer lesson could you wish.
No one forgets Fenisa's hook.
   Shh, someone knocked.

CELIA: Who's at the gate?   1830

FENISA: Go see if that cat-purse meowed.

[Tristan enters.]

TRISTAN: I hurried back, because I vowed
not to appear like an ingrate.
   Here's the money he sent me for.

FENISA: Let's see them. They're scudos for sure.   1835
Tristan, take this doubloon for your
trouble, and go tell your señor
   to come back and have lunch with me.
Tell him I'll be delighted to
see him. Go on, be off with you.   1840
I've got things to do here, you see.

TRISTAN:
[aside]   What comes on loan isn't worth that
much! I see bad signs in this house.
This time I think the little mouse
has snatched the money from the cat.   1845

[He exits.]

FENISA: He's gone?

CELIA: He went off muttering.

FENISA: And rivers murmur too; but when
the fish hear their music, then
they jump with happiness and sing.
   Do you suppose it would cause harm   1850
if I were to kiss this cat?

CELIA: No.
And it's a fat tabby cat, so
its purr gives pleasure, not alarm.

FENISA: You see Lucindo here in this?
Watch how I kiss him in this kitty.   1855

CELIA: Since any woman finds a pretty
lap dog acceptable to kiss,

| | Pues ¿por qué no besarás
un gato que es como un oro? | |
|---|---|---|
| Fenisa: | Yo lo diera a quien adoro. | 1860 |
| Celia: | No lo digas; loca estás. | |
| Fenisa: | Quiero a don Juan, que me pierdo. | |
| Celia: | Llama a este gato don Juan. | |
| Fenisa: | ¿Llaman? | |
| Celisa: | Sí, llamando están. | |
| Fenisa: | Pues con dinero me acuerdo
de amor, gran mal me apercibo.
Guarda este Lucindo en pelo. | 1865 |
| Celia: | Voy. | |
| Fenisa: | Cierra bien; que recelo
del alma de oro que es vivo. | |

[Vase Celia.]
El Capitán

| Capitán: | Después que vives ya tan recogida,
Fenisa, que a tu puerta y tu ventana
apenas hay un hombre que resida
un hora de la tarde o la mañana;
después que has dado en reducir tu vida
al estilo y manera valenciana,
ni admites juego ni conversa quieres:
¡qué bien medran con esto las mujeres!
   Solía yo ser tu galán de esquina,
el bravo de tu puerta y el matante,
el que echaba los hombres en cecina,
y de tu encantamiento era el gigante.
Ya duermes, como tímida gallina,
debajo de las alas de tu amante,
y antes que el sol acabe su carrera
no hay una mosca de tu puerta afuera.
   Estás enamorada, que parece
cosa imposible en condición tan loca.
¿Qué luto es éste y qué desdén que ofrece
tu vista y el silencio de tu boca?
¿Es don Juan, por ventura, el que merece
volver en agua tu cristal de roca?
Dame parte de todo como amigo. | 1870

1875

1880

1885

1890 |
|---|---|---|
| Fenisa: | Bien tengo, Capitán, que hablar contigo.
   Siempre al favor de tu española espada
en Sicilia viví, gallardo Osorio;
siempre, con libertad o enamorada,
mi pecho te mostré claro y notorio. | 1895 |

	what's wrong with you kissing a cat?	
	Especially one as good as gold.	
FENISA:	I'd give it to my love to hold.	1860
CELIA:	Don't tell me you're crazy as that?	
FENISA:	I'm lost in my love for Don Juan.	
CELIA:	Don Juan's calling this cat I fear.	
FENISA:	Someone's calling?	
CELIA:	Yes, can't you hear?	
FENISA:	With money, now I can go on	1865
	to love; and try not to get caught.	
	Keep this "Lucindo" tight in hand.	
CELIA:	I will.	
FENISA:	Take care: I understand	
	this heart of gold may be hard sought.	

[Celia exits.]
[Captain Osorio enters.]

OSORIO:	Fenisa, you've become such a recluse	1870
	that no one now can linger at your door;	
	your window grille is empty, you refuse	
	to let us stand there as we did before;	
	since you have chosen, sadly, to reduce	
	your life to the Valencian style, no more	1875
	do you play games, do you give us our say.	
	How do you women manage us this way?	
	I used to haunt the corner of your street.	
	The tough guy standing at your door was I.	
	I beat the men you wanted to be beat,	1880
	I was the giant shining in your eye.	
	Now you hide like a chicken in defeat:	
	beneath your lover's sheltering wings you lie.	
	Now before the sun sets, your door is bare:	
	not one man, not one fly can hang out there.	1885
	You seem to be in love, impossible	
	as that may be in one as wild as you.	
	What mourning clothes are these, what damnable	
	disdain? This silence and this frown are new.	
	Is it Don Juan who was so powerful	1890
	to change your crystal into tearful dew?	
	Please speak as friend, and stop my worrying.	
FENISA:	Good Captain, I will tell you everything.	
	'Til now, protected by your Spanish blade,	
	Osorio, I've lived here in Sicily	1895
	while, unattached or in my loving trade,	
	I've spoken to you fair and truthfully.	

Capitán:	Mira que traigo aquí una camarada,	
	no para alfeñicarse en locutorio,	
	sino para provecho de tu casa.	1900
Fenisa:	Pues suban todos, y hasta el dueño abrasa.	
Capitán:	¡Oh, soldados! ¿Qué digo? Ya hay licencia.	

Campuzano, Triviño y Orozco

Campuzano:	Beso a vuesamerced las manos.	
Triviño:	Todos nos remitimos hoy a su elocuencia.	
Fenisa: *[aparte]*	¿Españoles? Haránse de los godos.	1905
Orozco:	¿Hay sillas?	
Fenisa:	Celia...	
Campuzano:	Bueno en mi conciencia.	

Celia

Fenisa: *[aparte a Celia]*	¿Guardaste aquello?	
Celia:	Está cuarenta codos debajo de la tierra.	
Fenisa:	Bien has hecho.	
Celia:	¿Qué chusma es ésta? ¿Es gente de provecho?	
Fenisa:	Soldados y españoles, plumas, galas,	1910
	palabras, remoquetes, bernardinas,	
	arrogancias, bravatas y obras malas.	
Triviño:	Siempre me agradan estas francisquinas.	
Orozco:	¡Que siempre en agua de fregar resbalas!	
Triviño:	Vos sois poeta; allá cosas divinas...	1915
Orozco:	No sé, a fe de soldado, desta seta;	
	verdad es que en España fui poeta.	
Campuzano:	Y ¿érades vos de aquellos impecables,	
	cuyos versos destila en alambique	
	la culta musa?	
Orozco:	Fui de los palpables,	1920
	imitador de Laso y de Manrique.	

Osorio:	The comrade at my side was never made to foul the air with stupid courtesy, but rather to protect your house for you.	1900
Fenisa:	Come on in! Burn up the house, and me too!	
Osorio:	Hey, soldiers! Come inside. She says we can!	

Campuzano, Triviño and Orozco

Campuzano:	Please let me kiss your hand. We all today offer ourselves to serve you, every man.

Fenisa: [aside]	All Spaniards? Proud as Goths; see them make hay.	1905
Orozco:	Chairs?	
Fenisa:	Celia.	
Campuzano:	Not bad, for a courtesan.	

[Celia enters.]

Fenisa: [aside to Celia]	Did you guard that...?	
Celia:	I hid it well away, six feet under the ground.	
Fenisa:	I knew you would.	
Celia:	What riffraff is this? Will this do us good?	
Fenisa:	Spanish soldiers, bright clothes and feathered hats, hot words and joking, wisecracks and tall tales, strutting like peacocks, arguments and spats.	1910
Triviño:	I always liked frank doings in females.	
Orozco:	You always trip over the scrub girl's vats.	
Triviño:	You're such a poet: what divine details...	1915
Orozco:	By soldiers' faith: you mean you didn't know it? The truth is, back in Spain I was a poet.	
Campuzano:	And were you one of that unpleasant sect who cooked their cultist verse in a retort, 'til it turned into steam?	
Orozco:	No, you'd respect my verse; it was the Garcilaso sort.*	1920

---

*The popular fashion for convoluted, erudite and obscure Baroque poetry in the school of Luis de Góngora (1561-1627) was often contrasted to the more straightforward verses of Jorge Manrique (1440?-79) or Garcilaso de la Vega (1501-36).

CAPITÁN: Juguemos.

TRIVIÑO: Vengan dados.

CAPITÁN:
[aparte a Fenisa] Como entables
juego en tu casa, y español se pique,
habrá día que valga cien ducados,
y doscientos es poco.

CAMPUZANO: Traigan dados. 1925

[Van llegando un bufete; mete un escudero en una salvilla los dados, y comienzan a echar.]
Tristán

TRISTÁN:
[a Fenisa] ¿Puédote hablar?

FENISA: ¿Qué me quieres?

TRISTÁN: Mi señor queda a la puerta.

FENISA: ¿Qué quiere?

TRISTÁN: Comer, si acierta.
¡Graciosas sois las mujeres!
¿No le convidaste?

FENISA: ¿Yo? 1930

TRISTÁN: Luego ¿olvidaste, señora,
el concierto?

FENISA: Pues ¿ya es hora?

TRISTÁN: ¿Cómo es hora? La una dio.

FENISA: ¿La una?

TRISTÁN: ¡Bien, por mi vida!
¡Tras el gato falsos tratos! 1935
Pues cuando bajan los gatos,
suelen sacar la comida.

CAMPUZANO: Más a trece.

TRIVIÑO: Digo aquí.

CAMPUZANO: Aquesto más.

TRIVIÑO: Topo y tengo.

TRISTÁN: Yo no topo a lo que vengo. 1940
No lo habrá dicho por mí.

TRIVIÑO: Nueve, y diez, y trece.

CAMPUZANO: Bien.

OROZCO: Esto le corre detrás.

Osorio:	Let's play.
Triviño:	Bring on the dice.
Osorio: [aside to Fenisa]	If you protect gamblers, and these Spaniards start making sport, in one day you can make a hundred ducats. Bring on the dice.
Campuzano:	You'll soon have gold in buckets. 1925

[They bring in a writing desk; the squire puts the dice into a dice cup and they begin to throw.]
[Tristan enters.]

Tristan: [aside to Fenisa]	May I speak?	
Fenisa:	What do you want? Well?	
Tristan:	My lord is standing in the street.	
Fenisa:	What does he want?	
Tristan:	He wants to eat. You women really ring the bell! Didn't you ask him?	
Fenisa:	You mean me?	1930
Tristan:	My lady, you didn't forget the date?	
Fenisa:	Is it one o'clock yet?	
Tristan:	It just struck one. What lunacy!	
Fenisa:	Then it's one o'clock?	
Tristan:	What a bunch of nonsense: doesn't she know that after she has called out the cat it's customary to serve lunch?	1935
Campuzano:	I have thirteen.	
Triviño:	Then I'll play this.	
Campuzano:	Here is mine.	
Triviño:	Then I trump and win.	
Tristan:	I have no trump, to my chagrin, so what I'm trying for I miss.	1940
Triviño:	Nine, ten and thirteen.	
Campuzano:	Mine at last.	
Orozco:	Now look how far behind you fell.	

Tristán:	Si corriera el gato más, no le alcanzaran tan bien.	1945
Fenisa:	Dile, Tristán, a tu dueño que han venido estos soldados, todos hidalgos honrados, con mi enojo, y no pequeño; que me perdone, y me vea a la tarde.	1950
Tristán:	No hay en casa cosa que comer, y pasa la hora.	
Fenisa:	Dios le provea.	
Tristán:	¡Dios le provea! Pues ¿llega a puerta de algún convento?	1955
Fenisa:	Vete, Tristán.	
Campuzano:	Más.	
Tristán:	Reviento. ¡Ah, juventud loca y ciega!	
Fenisa:	¿Oyes?	
Tristán:	¿Qué?	
Fenisa:	Di que se venga esta tarde a merendar; que le quiero regalar.	1960
Tristán:	Para purgar se prevenga; que a fe que en esta respuesta no llevo mal testimonio.	
Fenisa:	Mira que hay aquí un demonio.	
Orozco:	La mitad me debéis désta.	1965
Tristán: *[aparte]*	Yo le llevo gentil lazo. Aunque discreto, cayó. El lindo gato le dio; mas ella lindo gatazo.	
[Vase.]		
Campuzano:	No juego más.	
Fenisa:	¿Quién ganó, para darle el parabién?	1970
Orozco:	Para qué barato os den mis manos y os sirva, yo.	
Capitán:	¿Tienes que comer?	

TRISTAN:	If our cat-purse had run that well they wouldn't have caught it so fast.	1945
FENISA:	Tell your master, Tristan, the blame is that soldiers arrived just then, all of them honored, noble men who have bothered me just the same. Ask him to forgive me: I'll be here this afternoon.	1950
TRISTAN:	We have no food anywhere in our house, so we'll starve.	
FENISA:	God will provide, you'll see.	
TRISTAN:	God will provide! Did he ordain us to beg at some convent door?	1955
FENISA:	Go now.	
CAMPUZANO:	I win.	
TRISTAN:	Boy, am I sore! Ah, youth! How blind, and how insane!	
FENISA:	Did you hear?	
TRISTAN:	What?	
FENISA:	Tell him to come this afternoon to take a bite with me. Then I will treat him right.	1960
TRISTAN:	He'll be lucky to find a crumb. I'll bear witness to what you've said, even though I don't like it much.	
FENISA:	Watch out, I've got a demon touch.	
OROZCO:	You owe me double; I'm ahead.	1965
TRISTAN: *[aside]*	She makes me take her net. He thought he'd belled the cat. But still he fell. He gave his cat-purse to this belle, and a clawing was all he got.	
[He exits.]		
CAMPUZANO:	I can't play any more.	
FENISA:	Who won? Well, whom should I congratulate?	1970
OROZCO:	I did, so I'm your fortunate servant in all; I am the one.	
OSORIO:	Is there food?	

Fenisa:	No falta.	
Orozco:	Celia, tomad esto vos.	1975
Capitán:	¿Hay criados?	
Fenisa:	Aquí hay dos.	
Capitán:	Vayan Cosmillo y Peralta y traigan cuatro capones, seis perdices, tres conejos.	
Triviño:	¿Y vino?	
Capitán:	Cuatro pellejos.	1980
Campuzano:	¿Fruta?	
Capitán:	Peras y melones.	
Fenisa:	Echa una pastilla aquí.	
Capitán:	No habéis visto la limpieza de Fenisa.	
Orozco:	Desta pieza ya lo demás presumí.	1985
Capitán:	Venid, y veréis su aseo, su pintura, estrado y cama.	
Triviño:	¡Por Dios, que es bizarra dama!	
Orozco: *[aparte a Osorio]*	Días ha que la deseo. Hablalda.	
Capitán:	Tened paciencia.	1990
Orozco:	No es posible que repose.	
Celia: *[a su ama]*	¿Qué hay de Lucindo?	
Fenisa:	Quedóse a la luna de Valencia.	

Vanse.
Lucindo y Tristán

Lucindo:	Pasaré con esta daga tu pecho.	
Tristán:	Pues yo, señor, ¿Qué culpa tengo, en rigor? ¿Qué quieres tú que le haga? ¿Qué tengo de responder, si estaban cuatro soldados coseletes?	1995

FENISA:	We have everything.	
OROZCO:	Celia, come here: this is for you.	1975
OSORIO:	Aren't there any servants?	
FENISA:	Yes, two.	
OSORIO:	Cosmillo and Peralta: bring some capons, partridges and hares: bring lots, make sure they're plentiful.	
TRIVIÑO:	And wine?	
OSORIO:	At least four wineskins full.	1980
CAMPUZANO:	And fruit?	
OSORIO:	Bring cantelopes and pears.	
FENISA:	I want you to burn some incense.	
OSORIO:	You've never seen such cleanliness as in Fenisa's house.	
OROZCO:	I'd guess that, if this room is evidence.	1985
OSORIO:	Come, look: her bathroom will amaze you, and her bedroom's something fine.	
TRIVIÑO:	Her wealth and style really shine!	
OROZCO: [aside to Osorio]	I have desired her for days. Speak to her.	
OSORIO:	Patience; I will soon.	1990
OROZCO:	How can I sit here quietly?	
CELIA:	Where's Lucindo?	
FENISA:	I've got him; he is lovesick, howling at the moon.	

[They exit.]
[A street]
Lucindo and Tristan

LUCINDO:	I'll take this knife and run you through if you don't...	
TRISTAN:	Sir, why do you scold? You can't blame me, if truth be told. What did you expect me to do? Tell me what was the proper line if the four soldiers there alarmed me so.	1995

Lucindo:	¿Cómo? ¿Armados?	2000

Tristán: Yo los vi resplandecer.
    Antes dije mil lisonjas,
viendo en dagas y en lanzones
más hierro por guarniciones
que a un locutorio de monjas. 2005
    Llega tú, llama y pregunta.
quizá el gato te dirá:
"hacia aquel desván está."

Lucindo: Llevo la color difunta.
    ¡Ah, mujer! Sospechas llevo 2010
que me has engañado.

Tristán: Pasa
de engaño. Es robo.

Lucindo:
[llamando]   ¡Ah de casa!

Celia, asomándose a una ventana

Celia: Pues ¿qué tenemos de nuevo?

Lucindo: Celia o infierno, ¿qué es esto
que hace tu ama conmigo? 2015

Celia: Pues ¿de qué se queja, amigo,
que viene tan descompuesto?
    ¡Jesús! ¿Infierno soy yo?

Lucindo: Llámame, Celia, ese cielo.
    Quizá me engaña el recelo 2020
que otras veces me engañó.

Celia: Está comiendo: no creo
que podrá salirte a hablar.

Lucindo: ¡Es buen modo de burlar
esto que a mis ojos veo! 2025
    ¿No era el convidado yo?

Fenisa, a la ventana

Fenisa: ¿Con quién habla? ¿Qué es aquesto?

Lucindo: ¡Mi vida!

Fenisa: ¿Quién es?

Lucindo: ¿Tan presto
de quién soy se te olvidó?

Fenisa: Soy algo corta de vista. 2030

LUCINDO:	Four soldiers! Were they armed?	2000
TRISTAN:	My own eyes saw the metal shine.	
	I tried lots of flattery, once	
	I'd seen so many pikes and swords.	
	There was more iron on those hordes	
	than round a convent full of nuns!	2005
	You go; knock on her door and ask.	
	See if the cat speaks truthfully:	
	"She's in that bedroom there, you see."*	
LUCINDO:	You've made me put on a death mask.	
	Ah, woman! Somehow I suspect	2010
	you have deceived me.	
TRISTAN:	This is more	
	than that; it's theft.	
LUCINDO: *[knocking]*	Open the door!	

Celia, looking out of the window

CELIA:	Something's up. Well, am I correct?	
LUCINDO:	You hellfiend, what is going on?	
	What's your mistress doing to me?	2015
CELIA:	My friend, why this antipathy?	
	What makes you look so pale and drawn?	
	And what makes me a fiend from Hell?	
LUCINDO:	Celia, call that heaven for me.	
	Am I fooled by her modesty	2020
	that fooled me once before so well?	
CELIA:	She's eating now; I don't believe	
	she can come out and talk with you.	
LUCINDO:	What a terrible thing to do!	
	My own eyes see how you decieve.	2025
	She invited me, after all.	

Fenisa at the window

FENISA:	What's this? Whom are you talking to?	
LUCINDO:	My life?	
FENISA:	Who is it?	
LUCINDO:	So soon you	
	forget? You really don't recall?	
FENISA:	I'm a bit nearsighted, that's all.	2030

---

*This appears to be a line from a popular song.

Lucindo:	Pues no se te echa de ver;	
	más que lince sueles ser	
	sin que un muro te resista.	
	¿Por qué tu vista condenas	
	más que a tus ojos ingratos,	2035
	pues es tal, que hasta los gatos	
	ves en las arcas ajenas?	
	Y cuando fueres tan corta	
	de vista, ¿no ha conocido	
	mi voz, Fenisa, tu oído?	2040
Fenisa:	Esa, Lucindo, reporta,	
	y ven esta noche acá;	
	que agora fue un accidente	
	el estar aquí esta gente.	
	Y no te espantes si está;	2045
	porque, como te pedí	
	el dinero que ya sabes	
	para ocasiones tan graves,	
	y me dijiste que sí,	
	y Tristán no le ha traído,	2050
	válgome de lo que puedo.	
Lucindo:	Agora me deja el miedo	
	desocupado el sentido.	
	Tristán, ¿que no se lo diste?	
Tristán:	¿Cómo no? ¡Qué lindo cuento!	2055
	Y lo metió en su aposento	
	Celia.	
Lucindo:	Pues ¿qué es esto? ¡Ay, triste!	
Fenisa:	¿Mandas otra cosa?	
Lucindo:	Escucha:	
	quede difinido aquí	
	cómo el dinero te di.	2060
Fenisa:	Tuvieras razón, y mucha,	
	si tú me le hubieras dado.	
[Entrase.]		
Lucindo:	Tristán, habla.	
Tristán:	Fuése ya.	
Lucindo:	¿Qué he de hacer?	
Tristán:	Que entres allá;	
	que yo me pondré a tu lado.	2065
	Todos españoles son,	
	y todos te han de ayudar.	
Lucindo:	Las puertas quiero quebrar.	

LUCINDO:	Go on! That's now what this man thinks.	
	When you want to be you're a lynx	
	who can see right through a stone wall.	
	Why is it your eyesight you're chiding	
	instead of your ingratitude?	2035
	You know your eyesight is so shrewd	
	that you can see a kitty hiding	
	in someone else's safe. You say	
	you're nearsighted, but can't you hear	
	my voice, Fenisa, in your ear?	2040
FENISA:	Lower your voice; now, go away.	
	Why don't you come back here tonight?	
	You know that it's an accident	
	these men are here. I never meant	
	to harm; but after all, it's right	2045
	that these men be here; because when	
	I asked you for the money for	
	that matter we discussed before,	
	and you told me you would, but then	
	Tristan never delivered it,	2050
	I had to find another way.	
LUCINDO:	I shake with fear at what you say;	
	your words have given me a fit.	
	Tristan: did you give her the money?	
TRISTAN:	You bet I did. That's all a lie!	2055
	And Celia hid it away. I	
	saw her.	
LUCINDO:	Oh! Something's awfully funny!	
FENISA:	Is there something else?	
LUCINDO:	Listen, wait.	
	Let's make one thing completely clear:	
	I did bring you the money here.	2060
FENISA:	You know I would not hesitate	
	to say that were true, if it were.	
[She exits.]		
LUCINDO:	Tristan, what now?	
TRISTAN:	She's gone inside.	
LUCINDO:	What shall I do?	
TRISTAN:	With me beside	
	you, let's go in there after her.	2065
	All those men are Spaniards in there:	
	they'll all help you settle the score.	
LUCINDO:	I am going to break down her door.	

[Llaman recio.]

TRISTÁN: Tienes enojo y razón.

Osorio, Campuzano, Orozco y Triviño, con las espadas desnudas

CAPITÁN: ¿Quién es el descomedido 2070
que, estando aquí honrada gente,
llama temerariamente?

LUCINDO: Yo, caballeros, no he sido.

CAPITÁN: Pues, ¿quién?

LUCINDO: Un paje, sospecho,
que cuatro platos traía. 2075

CAPITÁN: ¿Platos?

LUCINDO: Sí.

CAMPUZANO: ¿De quién sería?

CAPITÁN: De algún galán de provecho,
y como sintió el rüido,
se volvió.

CAMPUZANO: Discreto fue.

OROZCO: Vamos a comer; que a fe 2080
que fuera bien recibido.

[Vanse los soldados.]

LUCINDO: Con lindo anzuelo, con famoso estilo,
con ser un pez tan diestro, me ha burlado.
¡Qué bien que vuelvo a España despachado!
¡Qué bien me ha herido por el mismo filo! 2085
¡Ah, llanto del famoso cocodrilo!
Mi oído blandamente regalado,
a tus manos llegué, como engañado
peregrino de amor que pasa el Nilo.
  Dadme, cielos, venganza del anzuelo; 2090
desta mujer cruel quebrad la caña,
que es su artificio destrucción del suelo.
  Mirad que con sus lágrimas engaña,
mirad que vuelvo, en tanto desconsuelo,
lleno de amor y sin dinero a España. 2095

[Vase.]

TRISTÁN: Adiós, Sicilia; adiós, enredo isleño;
adiós, Palermo, puerto y franca puerta
a las naciones deste mundo abierta,
en quien tanta codicia rompe el sueño.
  Adiós, famoso gato, aunque pequeño. 2100
Vivo os quedáis, nuestra esperanza es muerta.
Pues no volvéis a España, cosa es cierta

[He pounds hard.]

TRISTAN: I think your anger's more than fair.

Osorio, Campuzano, Orozco *and* Triviño, *with their swords drawn*

OSORIO: Who is it that's so impolite 2070
that with these honored men in here
bangs on the door so free of fear?

LUCINDO: I'm not the fellow to indict.

OSORIO: Then who?

LUCINDO: Some page, who tried to take
some heavy dishes through, and fell. 2075

OSORIO: Dishes?

LUCINDO: Yes.

CAMPUZANO: Then whose page, pray tell.

OSORIO: Some young dandy who's on the make.
When he made so much noise, of course
he turned around.

CAMPUZANO: The fellow's rare.

OROZCO: Let's go have supper, for I swear 2080
I'm so hungry I'd eat a horse.

[The soldiers exit.]

LUCINDO: With hook so agile, and with famous style,
though I was clever, still this fish she caught.
She sends me home stripped clean of all I brought.
I got her, but she got to me meanwhile. 2085
She weeps just like the famous crocodile!
My ears her tender conversation sought,
I came to her as her deception taught:
love's pilgrim bravely venturing the Nile.
Heavens, I ask for vengeance on that hook: 2090
destroy that cruel woman's fishing pole
as she destroys the world, causing such pain.
See how her tears unleash deception; look;
see how, disconsolate, my lover's soul
broken from love, and broke, returns to Spain. 2095

[He exits.]

TRISTAN: Farewell to Sicily, and Island plot.
Farewell Palermo, frank and open port
where all the merchants of this world make sport,
and greed destroys what little sleep they've got.
Farewell, poor kitty, tiny little tot. 2100
You live, though our dead hopes you did abort.
You don't return to Spain, so the report

que no se muda el gato con el dueño.
      Adiós, Fenisa; adiós, gato del gato;
   adiós, cabo de Gata, cuyo espejo 2105
   puede servir de ejemplo y de recato.
      Pero permita Dios que tu pellejo
   antes de un mes, por tu bellaco trato,
   sirva de gato a un avariento viejo.

that cats move with their owners is pure rot.
    Goodbye, Fenisa, cat who caught the kitty.
Goodbye, Cape Cat, whose rocky crags are threat   2105
that we should take heed of and marvel at.
    May God unpeel your skin to make a pretty
cat-purse so you can be some miser's pet,
and thus repay your scheming tit for tat.

Jornada Tercera

Dinarda y Bernardo

DINARDA:	Pues ¿cómo vienes ansí?	2110
BERNARDO:	Estoy malo.	
DINARDA:	¿Tú? ¿De qué?	
BERNARDO:	No sé.	
DINARDA:	¿Cómo que no sé?	
BERNARDO:	Ni sé el mal, ni sé de mí.	
DINARDA:	¿Hate probado la tierra?	
BERNARDO:	Más el cielo me ha probado. ¡Ay, qué dolor que me ha dado! ¡Qué fuego mi pecho encierra! ¡Ay, ay! ¡Jesús, qué accidente! Tócame este pulso.	2115
DINARDA:	Muestra.	
BERNARDO:	Si es tanta la amistad nuestra, ponme la mano en la frente.	2120
DINARDA:	Ni el pulso, Bernardo, tiene movimiento extraordinario, ni más de aquel necesario calor a la frente viene.	2125
BERNARDO:	Tócame el rostro.	
DINARDA:	Ni en él tienes muestras de calor.	
BERNARDO:	¡Ay, qué terrible dolor! ¡Ay, qué dolor tan cruel!	
DINARDA:	¿Dónde?	
BERNARDO:	Al pecho se ha bajado; saltos me da el corazón.	2130
DINARDA:	Extraños dolores son.	
BERNARDO:	De extraña causa me han dado. Ponme la mano, así vivas, sobre el corazón.	
DINARDA:	Sí haré. Mas di al dolor que se esté quedo.	2135
BERNARDO:	Su accidente avivas. ¿No sientes que el corazón	

Act III

[Dinarda's Inn]
Dinarda and Bernardo

DINARDA: You're so mournful, you give me pause. 2110

BERNARDO: I'm sick.

DINARDA: And what makes you think so?

BERNARDO: I don't know.

DINARDA: How's that? You don't know?

BERNARDO: I don't know myself, or the cause.

DINARDA: Is it this land's got you depressed?

BERNARDO: Heaven's got me down even more. 2115
   Oh, what pain! Oh, I am so sore!
   What fire is burning in my chest!
     Oh, oh! Jesus, I think I'm dead!
   Put your hand on my pulse.

DINARDA: Let's see.

BERNARDO: If your friendship's that strong for me, 2120
   put your hand here on my forehead.

DINARDA: Bernardo, I feel your pulse beat
   exactly the way it ought to.
   From your forehead, I think that you
   have the normal degree of heat. 2125

BERNARDO: Touch my cheeks.

DINARDA: I can't ascertain
   that you have a fever at all.

BERNARDO: Worse agony I can't recall!
   Oh, what sharp, unbearable pain!

DINARDA: Where?

BERNARDO: It has gone down to my heart. 2130
   My heart is jumping in my breast.

DINARDA: That's a very strange pain at best.

BERNARDO: A strange reason caused it to start.
     If you love life, then put your hand
   over my heart.

DINARDA: All right, I will. 2135
   But you tell your pains to keep still
   then.

BERNARDO: Your touch makes my pains expand.
   Can't you feel how my heart explains

	te dice la causa dél?	
Dinarda:	Yo no siento nada en él.	2140
	Estos sus efectos son.	
Bernardo:	¿No te dice nada?	
Dinarda:	Nada.	
Bernardo:	¿Ni que eres tú quien le mueve?	
Dinarda:	¿Yo?	
Bernardo:	Tú, pues.	
Dinarda:	¿Cosa que lleve...?	
Bernardo:	Quedo, quedo. ¿Esto te enfada?	2145
Dinarda:	Luego ¿No me ha de enfadar	
	que me tengas por mujer?	

Fabio

Fabio:	¿Soy por acá menester?	
Bernardo:	Sí, porque quiere negar.	
Fabio:	¿Por qué niegas lo que ya	2150
	sabemos los dos?	
Dinarda:	¡Por Dios,	
	que es concierto de los dos!	
Fabio:	Así concertado está;	
	que sólo esperando estaba	
	que te defendieses dél.	2155
Dinarda:	¡Infames!	
Fabio:	No seas cruel;	
	deja invenciones, acaba.	
Bernardo:	Desde que entraste en la nave,	
	echamos todos de ver	
	que eras mujer.	
Dinarda:	¿Yo mujer?	2160
Bernardo:	Tú, pues.	
Dinarda:	¿Yo?	
Bernardo:	Fabio lo sabe.	
Dinarda:	Fabio, ¿qué has visto de mí?	
Fabio:	Lo que no he visto.	
Dinarda:	¡Villano!	
	Si pongo a la espada mano...	
Bernardo:	Detente.	

	what makes it hurt so painfully?	
DINARDA:	It says nothing at all to me. I think that it affects these pains.	2140
BERNARDO:	It tells you nothing?	
DINARDA:	Not a thing.	
BERNARDO:	Not even that you make it beat?	
DINARDA:	I?	
BERNARDO:	Of course, you.	
DINARDA:	That's really neat!	
BERNARDO:	Quiet. Why are we arguing?	2145
DINARDA:	Why shouldn't I be mad, if you let on I'm not what I appear?	

[Fabio enters.]

FABIO:	Say, am I needed around here?	
BERNARDO:	Yes, she wants to deny what's true.	
FABIO:	Well, why do you want to deny what we both know?	2150
DINARDA:	I can't tell whether the two of you planned this together.	
FABIO:	You're right: we planned it, he and I. We were only waiting to see you defend yourself from his arms.	2155
DINARDA:	You're incorrigible!	
FABIO:	No harm's done. Let's stop this idiocy.	
BERNARDO:	Since the day that the boat left shore everyone could tell that you were a woman.	
DINARDA:	Who, me? Are you sure?	2160
BERNARDO:	Yes, you.	
DINARDA:	Me?	
BERNARDO:	Fabio knows the score.	
DINARDA:	Fabio, what have you seen of me?	
FABIO:	What I haven't seen?	
DINARDA:	You're so crude. Don't make me draw my sword, if you'd...	
BERNARDO:	Hold on there!	

Dinarda:	¿Forzáisme aquí?	2165
Bernardo:	Somos muy mozos los dos para viejos de Susana.	
Dinarda:	¡Yo Susana!	
Fabio:	Cosa es llana en cuanto a mujer, ¡por Dios! Que de lo que es la inocencia era testimonio en ti.	2170
Bernardo:	¿Llaman?	
Fabio:	Sospecho que sí.	
Bernardo:	Perdí la ocasión.	
Fabio:	Paciencia.	

Fenisa y Celia

Fenisa:	¿Nunca he de ver yo tu casa?	
Dinarda:	¡Oh Fenisa! ¡Oh mi señora! ¡Oh amiga Celia! ¡Oh aurora del sol que el alma me abrasa! ¿En esta humilde posada tanto bien?	2175
Fenisa:	¿Adónde está el Capitán?	
Dinarda:	Salió ya.	2180
Fenisa:	Vengo, mi español, cansada de comprar cosas que son forzosas a las mujeres.	
Dinarda:	¿Quieres descansar, y quieres, por mi vida, colación?	2185
Fenisa:	La que tomara de ti, en la caja de esa boca la estoy mirando.	
Dinarda:	Era poca para servirte de mí el azúcar de Canaria, ni cuanto labran Valencia y Lisboa.	2190
Bernardo: *[aparte a Fabio]*	Una advertencia nos ha de ser necesaria. Ésta, ¿no ha venido aquí? Pues calla, y déjala hacer.	2195
Fenisa:	Deja, don Juan, de ofrecer,	

DINARDA:	You'd force me, I see?	2165
BERNARDO:	We're far too young to be the old men who Susana's bathing spied.	
DINARDA:	Me, Susana?	
FABIO:	As a girl I'd say you are, if the truth be told. But insofar as innocence, you claim it, but I just don't know.	2170
BERNARDO:	Is someone knocking?	
FABIO:	I think so.	
BERNARDO:	I lost my chance now.	
FABIO:	Have patience.	

Fenisa and Celia

FENISA:	Am I never to see your rooms?	
DINARDA:	Oh, Fenisa! My lady fair! Friend Celia! Dawn beyond compare of the sun who my soul consumes. These humble lodgings you've inspired with your grace.	2175
FENISA:	Let me ask about the Captain.	
DINARDA:	He long since went out.	2180
FENISA:	I come here, my Spanish friend, tired of shopping for the sort of thing women from time to time require.	
DINARDA:	You'd like to rest? Do you desire something to eat? What can I bring?	2185
FENISA:	The only sweet I want, I see on those sweet lips for which I yearn: that's my candy box.	
DINARDA:	Then you'd learn there are no sweets compared to me, not the sweetmeats from Grand Canary, not what my own Valencians make, nor even Lisboans.	2190
BERNARDO: *[aside to Fabio]*	To take note of all this is necessary. The woman's come here, hasn't she? Well, let her do what she came for.	2195
FENISA:	Don Juan, don't offer any more;	

pues es al revés en ti;
que lo ordinario es besar
y no ofrecer, y tu ofreces
y no besas.

DINARDA: Cuantas veces, 2200
Fenisa, voy a intentar
besar la imagen que amor
en su demanda me enseña,
luego me aparta y despeña
este siempre necio honor. 2205
Pero ¿quieres, por mi vida,
ver mi aposento y estancia,
donde no hay paños de Francia,
ni cama de oro vestida,
escritorios alemanes 2210
ni portugueses olores
sino los deseos mayores
y los gustos más galanes?

FENISA: Recíbolo a más amor
que si viera de Venecia 2215
el tesoro, o el que precia
Florencia de su señor.
Ni el Aranjüez de España
viera con más alegría.

DINARDA: Entra, dulce prenda mía. 2220

[*Vanse Dinarda y Fenisa.*]

BERNARDO:
[*aparte a Fabio*] ¿Van juntos?

FABIO: Sí.

BERNARDO: ¡Cosa extraña!
Ello es engaño sin duda,
pues requebrándose van.

FABIO: Por los indicios que dan,
Bernardo, de intento muda. 2225

BERNARDO: Mudaréle donde sé
de cierta ciencia que quiero
una mujer, y primero
de experiencia lo sabré.

FABIO: Mas ¿que me quieres hurtar 2230
el pensamiento, y que quieres
a Celia?

BERNARDO: Mi amigo eres;
y aunque me puedo enojar,
soy, Fabio, de parecer

	you do one opposite with me. What's normal is to give a kiss without offering, but you offer without kissing me.	

DINARDA:	I would proffer
	kisses, Fenisa, but when this
	   urge comes over me to embrace
	the image that love offers me
	then honor, that stupidity,
	tells me to remember my place.
	   But listen, would you like a tour
	of my parlor and sitting room?
	Not one tapestry of French loom,
	nor bedstead encrusted with pure
	   gold, nor table of German make
	nor Portuguese perfume will you
	find; rather, my desires will do
	instead, from them your pleasure take.
		2200
		
		2205
		
		2210

FENISA:	I am more honored to accept that than if you offered the treasure of Venice, or the fullest measure of goods that rich Florence has kept. Or even were you to arrange an Aranjuez of luxury.	2215
DINARDA:	My sweet delight, come in with me.	2220

[*Dinarda and Fenisa exit.*]

BERNARDO: [*aside to Fabio*]	They left together?	
FABIO:	Yes.	
BERNARDO:	That's strange! Something's going on with those two if they went off cooing that way.	
FABIO:	Bernardo, everything you say makes me think you are changing too.	2225
BERNARDO:	Next time I'll know for sure about whether I love a woman or not, because the next time, before I give my heart I'll try her out!	
FABIO:	Don't tell me, let me guess! I'll bet now you're going to say that you love Celia.	2230
BERNARDO:	You're my friend; because of that, Fabio, I won't get upset. In fact, I think together we	

                        que los dos la conquistemos;   2235
                        que yo sé que no seremos
                        muchos para una mujer.

[Cójenla en medio.]

FABIO: Celia...

BERNARDO: Celia...

CELIA: ¿Qué queréis?

FABIO: Yo te quiero.

BERNARDO: Yo te adoro.

FABIO: Yo me derrito.

BERNARDO: Yo lloro.   2240

CELIA: ¿Por tan libre me tenéis?

BERNARDO: Antes honrarte queremos.

CELIA: Los medios son bien honrosos.

BERNARDO: Somos extremos viciosos,
                y nuestra virtud te hacemos.   2245

Albano y Camilo

ALBANO: Aquí Fenisa entró.

CAMILO: Pues aquí vive
                el capitán Osorio, camarada
                de ese don Juan.

ALBANO: Sus pajes son aquéstos.

CAMILO: Y Celia aquélla.

ALBANO: ¡Oh Celia! ¡En esta casa!

CELIA: ¿Parécete milagro?

ALBANO: Dejo a Osorio   2250
                cuatro calles de aquésta, y no fue mucho
                tener a novedad que estéis en ella.

CELIA: Eso del capitán es cosa antigua.
                Las mujeres, Albano, y deste gusto,
                pican en novedades por momentos.   2255

ALBANO: Pues ¿que soldado vive aquí?

CELIA: ¡Oh, qué gracia!
                Vive la gentileza, la hermosura,
                la perla más preciosa que ha pasado
                de España a Italia; vive el mismo Adonis,
                de quien agora mi señora es Venus.   2260
                Vive don Juan de Lara.

		2235
	can overcome her reticence;	
	by twos we'll make twice as much sense;	
	we'll double her pleasure, you'll see.	

[They grab her between them.]

FABIO:	Celia...
BERNARDO:	Celia...
CELIA:	Let go of me!
FABIO:	I love you...
BERNARDO:	and I adore you.
FABIO:	I weep for you...
BERNARDO:	I'm crying too.	2240
CELIA:	How can you think that I'm that free?
BERNARDO:	To honor you is what he means.
CELIA:	The means you choose are really weird.
BERNARDO:	Extremes like us are to be feared.
	We'll make of you our golden mean.	2245

Albano and Camilo

ALBANO:	Fenisa went in here.
CAMILO:	This is the house of that Captain Osorio, who's the colleague of that Don Juan.
ALBANO:	Then these must be his pages.
CAMILO:	And that is Celia.
ALBANO:	Celia, in this house?
CELIA:	Well, what's so strange about that?
ALBANO:	I just left	2250
	Osorio four streets over, and you think that it's not strange I find you here so soon?
CELIA:	That business with the Captain's ancient stuff. Women, Albano, and especially that sort, demand new interests every day.	2255
ALBANO:	Then, what soldier lives here?
CELIA:	You're very funny. Gentility lives here, and loveliness, the most exquisite pearl that ever passed to Italy from Spain; here lives Adonis, for whom my lady Venus has become.	2260
	Here lives Don Juan de Lara.

CAMILO:
[aparte a Albano] ¿Qué os parece?
¿Será agora mujer don Juan de Lara?

ALBANO: Celia, espera por Dios; escucha, Celia.
¿Fenisa con don Juan?

CELIA: Deja los celos
del Capitán, que nunca amó Fenisa, 2265
y cree que don Juan la tiene loca.

ALBANO: ¡Fenisa y don Juan dices que se hablan!
Y ¿los has visto juntos?

CELIA: Yo lo digo,
y aun tú lo puedes ver.

ALBANO: ¡Válgame el cielo!

CAMILO: Albano, si en las cosas que se dudan 2270
no habemos de dar crédito a los ojos,
¿qué probanza nos queda más segura?
Dejad aqueste loco pensamiento;
que don Juan no es Dinarda, vuestra dama,
ni lo ha de ser por fuerza.

ALBANO: Agora digo 2275
que no es milagro en la naturaleza
la extraña diferencia de los rostros.
Yo estoy desengañado.

CELIA: Mira, Albano,
si mandas otra cosa.

ALBANO: Dios te guarde.

CELIA: Mi señora me llama.

BERNARDO: Y a nosotros 2280
don Juan.

FABIO: Hoy, Celia, has de quedar por mía.

BERNARDO: Y de los dos.

CELIA: ¡Qué tierna me han hallado!

BERNARDO: Bien caben muchas bestias en un prado.

[Vanse Celia, Bernardo y Fabio.]

CAMILO: ¿Resta averiguar alguna cosa
en razón de si aqueste caballero 2285
es hombre, y hombre que Fenisa adora?

ALBANO: A lo menos, Camilo, me ha servido
este retrato de Dinarda bella
de alborotarme el alma de tal modo,
que ha borrado la estampa de Fenisa. 2290

CAMILO:
[aside to Albano]   Well, now what?
You still think Juan de Lara is a woman?

ALBANO: Celia, for the love of God; Celia, wait.
Fenisa's with Don Juan?

CELIA: Yes, you can quit
being jealous of the Captain, for she never
loved him, while Juan de Lara drives her wild.

ALBANO: You say Fenisa and Don Juan are talking?
You've seen them both together?

CELIA: Yes I have,
and you can see them too.

ALBANO: May God forbid.

CAMILO: Albano, if when we're unsure of things,
we refuse to give credit to our eyes,
how can we find a proof better than that?
Forget this crazy mania of yours:
Don Juan is not Dinarda, not your lady,
and won't be, though you try to force it.

ALBANO: Now
I say there is no miracle in how
Dame Nature varied everybody's faces.
No more am I deceived.

CAMILO: Albano, tell
me what else you might need.

ALBANO: God keep you well.

CELIA: My lady's calling me.

BERNARDO: And our Don Juan
is calling us.

FABIO: Now you belong to me.

BERNARDO: To both of us.

CELIA: What do you think I am?

BERNARDO: In one field lots of animals can graze.

[Exit Celia, Bernardo and Fabio.]

CAMILO: Have we still got things left to figure out?
Since now we're sure this person is a man,
a man, moreover, whom Fenisa loves?

ALBANO: At the very least, Camilo, this portrait
of the beautiful Dinarda has served
to unsettle my soul to such extent
that it's erased the picture of Fenisa.

[*Vanse Albano y Camilo.*]
Albano y Camilo, en la calle

CAMILO: No de otra suerte que la sombra huye
al resplandor del sol, o la mentira
cuando se prueba la verdad gloriosa,
huyó Fenisa, que era amor fingido,
a la luz del retrato de Dinarda, 2295
y quedastes, Albano, de su engaño
libre: piedad que le debéis al cielo,
porque desde el primero movimiento
de sus divinos tornos, hasta el último
que han dado sus esferas celestiales, 2300
no se ha visto mujer tan engañosa.

ALBANO:
[*viendo venir gente*] Forasteros son éstos.

CAMILO: Y españoles.

ALBANO: A la cuenta, no ha mucho que salieron
del mar.

CAMILO: De almacenar su hacienda vienen.

ALBANO: Vamos de aquí.

CAMILO: ¡Qué buenos talles tienen! 2305

[*Vanse.*]
Lucindo, Tristán, don Félix y Donato

DON FÉLIX: El amistad de un camino
tan largo, y haber hallado
en vos pecho tan honrado
y entendimiento divino,
  Lucindo, no me permite 2310
ni dejaros, ni dejar
de daros parte y lugar
adonde a nadie se admite,
  que es lo que un alma atesora.
Lo que en la nave encubrí 2315
desde Vinaroz aquí,
quiero que sepáis agora...
  Retírate allá, Donato.

LUCINDO: Desvíate allá, Tristán.

DON FÉLIX: Leyes del mundo, que van 2320
donde quiere el tiempo ingrato,
  Lucindo, mi edad mejor
en su sazón han cortado,
como suele el tosco arado
llevar de paso la flor. 2325

[Exit Albano and Camilo.]
Albano and Camilo in the street

CAMILO: The same way that the shadow flees the splendor
of the sun, the same way that falsehood flees
when glorious truth is proved for all to see,
so fled Fenisa, for her love was false,
before the shining portrait of Dinarda. 2295
And you, at last, remained, Albano, free
from her deceptions; you ought to give thanks
to the heavens, for from the very first
of its divine movements until the last
circuit that's made by the celestial spheres, 2300
there's never been such a deceitful woman.

ALBANO:
*[He sees people
coming.]* These men are foreigners.

CAMILO: I think they're Spaniards.

ALBANO: From the looks of them they must have just come
from the sea.

CAMILO: They come from storing their goods.

ALBANO: Come on, let's go.

CAMILO: They're a good-looking bunch. 2305

[They exit.]
Lucindo, Tristan, Don Felix and Donato

FELIX: Since we've become friends on this trip
I know you have honor; I've found
your judgment has always been sound.
As you have nurtured our friendship,
   Lucindo, I cannot leave you 2310
now; and more, I want to invite
you into that place I've kept tight
from all but a most select few:
   I'm speaking of my inner soul.
The news that I kept hidden close 2315
on our journey from Vinaroz
now I want to tell you: the whole
   thing. Donato, you move away.

LUCINDO: Tristan, you go over there too.

FELIX: The laws of this world, which are true 2320
whenever thankless time holds sway,
   Lucindo, the best years of my
life have trampled down in their season
the way the rough plow, without reason,
kills flowers as it slices by. 2325

	Yo vengo a matar un hombre a Sicilia.	
Lucindo:	Habéisme honrado en no haberme despreciado por la humildad de mi nombre; que siendo don Félix vos, caballero sevillano, yo mercader valenciano, tan desiguales los dos, debo estimar con razón que me tratéis como amigo.	2330

2335 |
Don Félix:	Bien veréis en lo que os digo si os he dado el corazón.	
Lucindo:	Para que no presumáis que no estimo esa merced, que os quiero pagar creed, aunque de mi amor lo estáis. ¿Vos a Sicilia venís a matar un hombre?	2340
Don Félix:	Vengo a matar un hombre, y tengo razón.	
Lucindo:	Muy bien advertís. Yo vengo a tomar venganza de una mujer, y también tengo razón.	2345
Don Félix:	Si de quien hizo de vos confianza, Lucindo, tenerse puede, mirad si puedo ayudaros.	2350
Lucindo:	Querría el caso contaros, si el tiempo lugar concede. Yo vine a Palermo, habrá dos meses, y una mujer fingió quererme.	2355
Don Félix:	¿Querer saben?	
Lucindo:	Olvídanlo ya. Regalóme, fingió estar enamorada de mí; que el anzuelo en que caí, pudiera entonces pescar al más severo Catón, al más recatado estilo; porque es aquí un cocodrilo	2360

	I've come to Sicily to kill
	a man.
LUCINDO:	You've greatly honored me
	by not treating me shabbily
	or taking my low birth for ill.
	Even though you, Don Felix, are	2330
	a *caballero* from Seville,
	I a Valencian merchant, still
	we two cannot be on a par.
	Which is why I'm so pleased you treat
	me so completely like a friend.	2335
FELIX:	In what I say you'll comprehend
	that now our hearts beat with one beat.
LUCINDO:	Thank you for the magnitude of
	this courtesy you've shown me. You
	can be certain I will be true	2340
	as you can be sure of my love.
	Then you have come to Sicily
	to kill a man?
FELIX:	I have indeed.
	And never did a person need
	killing more. Right's on my side.
LUCINDO:	We	2345
	are together. I also came
	to take vengeance on a girl who
	wronged me, and right is with me too.
FELIX:	My trust in you should be the same
	as yours in me. This is the stuff	2350
	of friendship. Let me help you out.
LUCINDO:	I'll tell you everything about
	the case if there is time enough.
	Two months ago, when I first got
	here a woman falsely spoke love	2355
	to me.
FELIX:	Do women still know of
	love then?
LUCINDO:	If they did, they forgot.
	She showered me with gifts, and she
	pretended love in all that followed.
	I tell you that the hook I swallowed	2360
	is such that it would have neatly
	fished up even Cato the wise,
	or anyone else of that style.
	What with her deadly crocodile

                que llora y mata a traición.   2365
                    Es entre dama y señora,
                entre cortesana y grave,
                que sabe engañar, y sabe
                ser firme hasta que enamora.
                    De allí abajo no hay amor,   2370
                porque a quien ha de querer,
                o ha de ser otra mujer,
                o tratalla con rigor.
                    El anzuelo con que pesca,
                es regalar al que coge,   2375
                para que después se arroje.

Don Félix: ¡Linda treta!

Lucindo: Linda y fresca.
                    Halléla en su casa un día
                con más luto que una mula
                canóniga...

Don Félix: ¡Cuánto adula   2380
                una falsa cortesía!

Lucindo: Dióme una carta, de suerte
                que vi en ella que quedaba
                preso su hermano, y que estaba,
                Félix, sentenciado a muerte;   2385
                    mas que por dos mil ducados
                la parte perdonaría.
                Esto fue porque sabía,
                o de mí o de mis criados,
                    que yo tenía el dinero   2390
                de lo que había vendido.
                No vi este gato fingido,
                y dísele verdadero,
                    porque con joyas y prendas
                me quería asegurar;   2395
                mas no las quise tomar.

Don Félix: Necedad.

Lucindo: Muy bien enmiendas.
                    De allí adelante se fue
                secando, y no poco a poco;
                yo a su reja y puerta loco   2400
                algunas noches pasé.
                    Negó el dinero; entendí
                cobrarlo, y era sacar
                una sortija del mar.
                Cuando el imposible vi,   2405
                    volvíme a Valencia, donde
                no fui muy bien recibido,
                de donde agora he venido

	tears, she can kill you with her cries.	2365
	She's half lady and half grand dame,	
	half courtly and half courtesan,	
	who knows how to deceive a man	
	with love until he feels the same.	
	From then on there's no love at all;	2370
	for the only type her kind can	
	love is a woman, or a man	
	who mistreats her to make her fall.	
	The hook that she uses to catch	
	men is to give them gifts so fine	2375
	that they throw themselves at her line.	
FELIX:	Clever!	
LUCINDO:	Clever and without match.	
	One day I found her in her house	
	decked out in more black clothing than	
	a priest's mule.	
FELIX:	Oh what false hope can	2380
	pretense of courtesy arouse!	
LUCINDO:	She showed me a letter where I	
	read about her brother who had	
	been made prisoner, and that the lad,	
	Felix, had been condemned to die.	2385
	And for only two thousand gold	
	ducats, the injured party would	
	forgive him. That number she could	
	have known because my servant told	
	her, or else I did, that the city	2390
	for all our goods had paid us that	
	amount. I missed what a false cat	
	she was, so I gave her the kitty.	
	She wanted to secure the loan	
	with some jewels and things she'd kept,	2395
	but I didn't want to accept.	
FELIX:	Too bad!	
LUCINDO:	Your feelings match my own.	
	If up 'til then all had been right,	
	from there things went quickly downhill:	
	I at her door and windowsill,	2400
	crazy, waiting there the whole night.	
	When I asked her about the money,	
	she claimed that she hadn't a notion.	
	Finding a lost ring in the ocean	
	was easier! That's enough funny	2405
	business. So I sailed back home, where	
	I was not well received at all.	
	So I've come back to try to call	

	para ver si corresponde	
	la venganza al pensamiento;	2410
	que esta hacienda que registro,	
	no es más de porque al registro	
	acuda este lobo hambriento.	
	Cuanto saqué de la nave,	
	y metí en el aduana,	2415
	fue ostentación tan liviana,	
	que apenas en ella cabe,	
	y no vale cien escudos.	
Don Félix:	Así mi desdicha fuera;	
	que como hacienda perdiera,	2420
	ella y yo fuéramos mudos.	
Lucindo:	¿Es honra?	
Don Félix:	No es menos prenda.	
Lucindo:	Sí; pero habéis de saber	
	que en cualquiera mercader	
	es honra también la hacienda.	2425
	Tras el caudal, si se pierde,	
	va el crédito, pues perdido...	

[Hablan bajo.]
Fenisa y Celia

Celia:	Pues ¿no me dirás qué ha sido?	
Fenisa:	Nadie, Celia, me lo acuerde.	
	Nadie me nombre a don Juan.	2430
	El que le abriere mi puerta,	
	no la verá más abierta.	
Celia:	¡Jesús! ¿Lucindo y Tristán?	
Fenisa:	¡Válame Dios! ¿No era ido?	
Celia:	Fuése y ha vuelto.	
Fenisa:	¿A qué viene?	2435
Celia:	Vino a ese trato que tiene.	
	¿Si te habrá puesto en olvido?	
Fenisa:	Los hombres, Celia, no olvidan	
	adonde los tratan mal;	
	que es condición natural	2440
	porfiar donde despiden.	
	Si de don Juan no viniera	
	tan mohina, aquí le hablara.	
Celia:	Pues ¿qué fue aquesto?	
Fenisa:	"Repara,	

	in what's owed me, and to prepare	
	a vengeance equal to my hate.	2410
	The goods I brought now, everything	
	is for just one purpose: to bring	
	this hungry she-wolf to the bait.	
	What I unloaded from my boat	
	into the Customs Shed was stuff	2415
	of little substance, just enough	
	so that the boxes wouldn't float,	
	a hundred scudos worth at most.	
FELIX:	Would my misfortune were so small!	
	For if my possessions were all	2420
	I'd lost, I'd be dumb as a post.	
LUCINDO:	Is it honor then?	
FELIX:	Nothing less.	
LUCINDO:	All right, but you must realize	
	that for a merchant honor lies	
	in his merchandise, his business.	2425
	For once you lose your capital	
	you lose your credit too, and then...	

[They go on speaking softly.]
Fenisa and Celia

CELIA:	Tell me what the trouble has been.	
FENISA:	Nobody, Celia, may recall	
	to me the name of that Don Juan.	2430
	Whoever lets him through my door	
	will never see it open more.	
CELIA:	Jesus! Lucindo and Tristan?	
FENISA:	Good God! I thought he had departed.	
CELIA:	He went and he came back.	
FENISA:	To do	2435
	what?	
CELIA:	Unless he's forgotten you,	
	to finish the business you started.	
FENISA:	Men, Celia, don't ever forget	
	when someone's done them a wrong turn;	
	it's natural that when you spurn	2440
	them they try to repay the debt.	
	If I weren't so upset about	
	Don Juan, I'd go speak to him there.	
CELIA:	What happened?	
FENISA:	The old song: "Take care,	

	mira, advierte, considera,	2445
	lo que dirá el Capitán…";	
	y tras esto, me ha rogado	
	que diga que me ha gozado.	
Celia:	Los dos mirándote están.	
Lucindo: [aparte a don Félix]	¡Ay, don Félix! ésta es la causa de mis enojos.	2450
Fenisa: [a Lucindo]	¿Sabes algo destos ojos? ¿Qué es lo que en sus niñas ves?	
Lucindo:	Sé que esas niñas lo son de manera en la mudanza, que dan menos esperanza después de la posesión.	2455
Fenisa:	Suelen los recién venidos abrazar los bien hallados.	

Lucindo:	Bien venidos tan cansados
	siempre son mal recibidos.
	  Pagástete de tu mano,
	no fiando de la mía
	en la mayor niñería
	que pudo un pecho liviano.
	  Sabe Dios que no sentí
	perder, Fenisa, el dinero,
	mas ver mi amor verdadero,
	y verle fingido en ti;
	  que con dar vuelta a Valencia,
	adonde hay padres honrados,
	traigo treinta mil ducados.
		2460
		
		2465
		
		2470

Fenisa:	Tienes tú poca paciencia.
	  Yo sólo quise probarte.
	Confieso que recibí
	el dinero, y me escondí
	en la mira de adorarte.
	  Gusté de escuchar tus quejas,
	porque oyendo sus extremos,
	porque no nos arrojemos
	tienen las ventanas rejas.
	  El día que te partiste,
	con Celia envié a llamarte.
	Acababas de embarcarte.
	¡Qué buena noche me diste!
	  ¡Qué lágrimas me costó
	haber querido, y querer
		2475
		
		2480
		
		2485

	consider, be certain, watch out,	2445
	think of what the Captain might say..."	
	Beyond that, he asked me to tell	
	people he's slept with me as well.	
CELIA:	Now those two are looking this way.	
LUCINDO: [aside to Don Felix]	Look, Don Felix. She's the one. She	2450
	is the cause of my painful sighs.	
FENISA: [to Lucindo]	What do you know about these eyes?	
	In my pupils what do you see?	
LUCINDO:	Pupils?! They're grown up women, they	
	change their manner so rapidly;	2455
	they give less hope of things to be	
	once they've got firm hold on their prey.	
FENISA:	I thought you newcomers embraced	
	the good things you find when you come.	
LUCINDO:	But a welcome that tiresome	2460
	always leaves you a bitter taste.	
	You took it on yourself to take,	
	not willing to trust my largesse,	
	in the worst proof of foolishness	
	that an inconstant heart could make.	2465
	The loss of cash was not what pained	
	me most, Fenisa, about you,	
	but to see that my love was true,	
	and to see that your love was feigned.	
	I went home for new goods, more than	2470
	before. My parents, of high birth,	
	gave thirty thousand ducats worth.	
FENISA:	You are such an impatient man!	
	I only wanted to test you.	
	I got the money, I admit	2475
	that. Then I lay low to permit	
	me to watch what my love would do.	
	I liked hearing you moan so hard;	
	though when your grief was extreme I	
	thought I'd kill myself; I know why	2480
	it is that our windows are barred.	
	The day you left, you must believe,	
	I sent Celia to make you stay.	
	But you'd already sailed away:	
	that was no way to take your leave.	2485
	Oh, what tears you cost me. The more	
	I adored you, the more I would	

                probarte!

Don Félix:
[aparte]   ¡Astuta mujer!

Lucindo:
[aparte]   Desta suerte me engañó.

Fenisa:
      No sé cómo te refiero   2490
aquel dolor desigual.
Solamente en tanto mal
me consoló tu dinero.
      Aquella prenda tomaba
en las manos, y decía   2495
cosas que quien las oía
enternecida quedaba.

Lucindo:
      ¿Es posible, mi señora,
que merecí con mi ausencia
lágrimas tuyas? Paciencia.   2500
Necio fui, súpelo agora.
      ¡Vive Dios, que si en la mar
esa nueva me llegara,
que a las aguas me arrojara,
y te volviera a buscar!   2505
      En la calle estás, mi bien:
no es justo tenerte aquí.
Si tú me quieres así,
yo te quiero así también.
      Patria y padres, perdonad;   2510
no ha de volver del dinero
a Valencia escudo entero.
¿Entero? Ni la mitad.
      Ve, Fenisa, a la Aduana,
infórmate si he traído   2515
hacienda, y por Dios te pido,
de esa beldad soberana,
      que en vendiéndola te entregues
en la plata y en el oro,
pues me basta por tesoro   2520
que mirarte no me niegues.
      ¿Podréte agora abrazar?

Fenisa: Agora y siempre, mi bien.

Lucindo:
    Vete con Dios, y prevén
para esta noche lugar;   2525
      que voy con aqueste hidalgo
en casa de un mercader,
que merced me quiere hacer,
por él, no por lo que valgo,
      de que a cambio se me den   2530
tres mil ducados, en tanto

try to test you.

FELIX:
[aside]   This woman's good!

LUCINDO:
[aside]   That's how she deceived me before.

FENISA: I cannot tell you the frustration   2490
I was feeling with such sharp grief.
Nowhere could I turn for relief;
though your money was consolation.
    I took that remembrance in my
two hands and such sweet things I said   2495
that whoever heard would be led
to moan with me and weep and sigh.

LUCINDO: My lady, can it really be
that my absence sufficed to wring
tears from you? Be patient; the thing   2500
is just now coming clear to me.
    By heaven, if that news had reached
me out at sea I would have flung
myself into the waves to come
find you again on this fair beach.   2505
    My love, we're standing in the street;
it's not right to talk to you here.
If you love me this much, my dear,
then I love you the same, my sweet.
    Forgive me, parents and homeland;   2510
my Valencia will never see
this cash in its entirety.
If half survives it will be grand!
    Go to the Customs Shed, and make
certain, Fenisa, that I've got   2515
exactly what I said I brought;
then I beg, for your beauty's sake,
    that when you've seen it you'll be won
over by my silver and gold.
My real treasure, if truth be told,   2520
is that you do not hide your sun.
    And now is an embrace all right?

FENISA: Right now, and whenever you care.

LUCINDO: Go with God, my love, and prepare
a good welcome for me tonight.   2525
    Right now we are going to see
a merchant here about a loan:
for my friend's sake, and not my own,
he's doing this favor for me.
    He's going to give me three thousand   2530
ducats until I sell the stuff

	que vendo...	
Fenisa:	De ti me espanto. ¿No era yo buena, mi bien, para negociar las cosas de tu gusto?	
Lucindo:	Pues ¿tendrías quién me los diese?	2535
Fenisa:	Estos días ciertas doncellas hermosas a un capitán han hablado que tiene ciertos escudos, que están suspensos y mudos sin provecho y con cuidado. A cambio te los darán. ¿Para qué son?	2540
Lucindo:	Para trigo; que hay falta allá.	
Fenisa:	Espera, amigo; que éstas te acomodarán.	2545
Lucindo:	De aquesta mercadería que traigo, hay agora acá, y si la vendo, será con poca ganancia mía. Si aguardo un mes, ganaré la mitad por medio, y quiero, tomando aqueste dinero, aunque pierda, pues podré desquitallo en la ganancia, fletar la nave.	2550
Fenisa:	Harás bien, y yo haré que te le den. Pero, ¿será de importancia el resguardo de tu hacienda?	2555
Lucindo:	Del almacén en que está daré las llaves.	
Fenisa:	Será, Lucindo, bastante prenda.	2560
Lucindo:	Para tener más lugar de estar contigo, no quiero vender tan presto, y espero que te sabré regalar.	2565
Fenisa:	Harto regalo me ofreces con verte, dulce bien mío. ¿Pagarásme?	

	I've brought.	
FENISA:	My love, I've heard enough!	
	You know you have me here at hand	
	to help you obtain what you must	
	have to do your business with.	
LUCINDO:	Why, do you know of a...?	2535
FENISA:	Some of my most beautiful girl friends have just talked with a certain captain who has certain scudos which are not earning interest, and that has got the poor old captain in a stew. I'm certain you could get a loan. Why do you need it?	2540
LUCINDO:	To buy some wheat, which they need there.	
FENISA:	But why come borrowing? Why not sell your own?	2545
LUCINDO:	The goods I bring you have no need of here right now; there's a supply already, and if I sell I will get very little indeed. But if I wait a month, I can earn half again as much or more. That's what I want this money for. Even though it costs me, I plan to get it all back when I sell, and fill up my boat.	2550
FENISA:	Good for you. I'll make sure that the loan goes through. But say, will you mind if I tell him your goods will secure the loan?	2555
LUCINDO:	If he wants it, the warehouse key is his.	
FENISA:	And that's security enough for anyone, I'd own.	2560
LUCINDO:	To have more time to spend with you I'm willing to wait to sell my goods for a long while. That way I can love you and favor you too.	2565
FENISA:	Seeing you is enough to serve as favor, my love. Will you give me something?	

Lucindo:	Yo confío pagarte como mereces.	
Fenisa:	Advierte que han de querer treinta por ciento.	2570
Lucindo:	Eso es cosa cruel.	
Fenisa:	Pues será forzosa.	
Lucindo:	No es razón.	
Fenisa:	Esto ha de ser.	
Lucindo:	Tú negocia que sean veinte, por vida de aquestos ojos. Mas no quiero darte enojos, mi alma; que pasa gente. Yo te iré a ver esta tarde. Habla a Fenisa, Tristán.	2575

[Lucindo habla con don Félix.]

Fenisa:	¡Tristán, qué bueno y galán!	2580
Tristán:	Señora, el cielo te guarde.	
Fenisa:	Ya, como ricos venís, hablaréis por petición.	
Tristán:	Otra ha sido la ocasión.	
Fenisa:	Ya sé lo que presumís.	2585
Tristán:	¡Ojalá presunción fuera! No es sino pura verdad. ¡Mal haya la voluntad que en quererte perservera! Habiéndole tú engañado, viene este tonto a querer a la más falsa mujer.	2590
Fenisa:	¡Tristán!	
Tristán:	Estoy enojado. ¡Si vieras al moscatel en la mar, lleno de fuego, por hallar algún sosiego querer arrojarse en él! ¡Si le vieras en Valencia llorar hasta que juntó tanta hacienda y se embarcó!... Pensé perder la paciencia.	2595 2600
Fenisa:	¿Trae mucha?	
Tristán:	Trae casi nada:	

Lucindo:	I swear, as I live, that I'll give you what you deserve.	
Fenisa:	I warn you that he'll try to hit you for thirty percent.	2570
Lucindo:	That's not right.	
Fenisa:	No, but that's what you have got.	
Lucindo:	That's unfair.	
Fenisa:	There's no help for it.	
Lucindo:	You try to get twenty, my sweet; for my sake see what you can do. —But I don't want to bother you, love; there are people in the street. I'll come see you later today. Go talk to Fenisa, Tristan.	2575

[Lucindo talks with Don Felix.]

Fenisa:	Tristan: my, aren't you getting on.	2580
Tristan:	May the Lord keep you safe, I pray.	
Fenisa:	Now that you come here like rich men, you use those pompous formulas.	
Tristan:	That's not the only thing there was.	
Fenisa:	I know what you're assuming then.	2585
Tristan:	Assuming! Worse than that I fear. No; every word of it is true. Whoever falls in love with you is damned if he should persevere. You thoroughly deceived the lad and the stupid oaf took a dive for the falsest woman alive!	2590
Fenisa:	Tristan!	
Tristan:	I'm sorry, but I'm mad! If you had witnessed what emotion this novice burned with out at sea; trying to find tranquility, he nearly jumped into the ocean! Back in Valencia he was grim, moaning all the time he was getting his new goods together and setting sail! I near lost patience with him.	2595 2600
Fenisa:	Did he bring much?	
Tristan:	Not very much.	

treinta mil ducados son.

FENISA: Probar quise su afición.
Su hacienda tengo guardada. 2605

TRISTÁN: Ahora bien, gaste su hacienda,
vaya a tu casa esta vez,
dé a sus padres tal vejez,
cumpla bien con su encomienda;
que con no volver a España 2610
con él, habré yo cumplido.

FENISA: Tristán, no me has conocido.

TRISTÁN: Conozco quién es la caña
adonde prendió el anzuelo
que aquel gato nos pescó. 2615

FENISA: ¡Qué vestido te hice yo
de un famoso terciopelo,
con mil pasamanos de oro,
que por irte le perdiste!

TRISTÁN: ¿Vestido ¡por Dios! me hiciste? 2620

FENISA: ¡Qué linda cosa!

TRISTÁN: Eso ignoro:
pues tentado de galán,
yo te llevaré este loco,
que no ha de valerte poco.

FENISA: Si me le llevas, Tristán, 2625
el vestido y cien ducados
son tuyos.

TRISTÁN: Beso tus pies.

FENISA: Adiós.

CELIA: Adiós.

LUCINDO:
[a don Félix] Ésta es
la ocasión de mis cuidados.

FENISA: Mira, mi bien, que te espero. 2630

LUCINDO: Haz el dinero traer.

FENISA: Pues advierte que ha de ser
treinta por ciento el dinero.

LUCINDO: Como quisieres.

CELIA:
[aparte a Fenisa] ¿A quién
lo piensas pedir?

	Thirty thousand ducats at best.	
FENISA:	I wanted to put him to test. I've got all his things safe from touch.	2605
TRISTAN:	Then let him spend all he has brought; let him use your house for his stage; let him wreck his parents' old age; let him fulfill what he's been taught. For by not going back to Spain I too will have fulfilled my call.	2610
FENISA:	Tristan, you don't know me at all.	
TRISTAN:	I know who holds the fishing cane, and I know who wiggles the hook that managed to catch our fat kitty.	2615
FENISA:	I had made for you such a pretty velvet suit, all the newest look, with a thousand spangles of gold. You lost it by going away!	
TRISTAN:	By God, you had clothes made, you say?	2620
FENISA:	They were nice.	
TRISTAN:	Why wasn't I told? Well then, I'll bring you this madman, since you've tempted me with fine clothes, and you'll gain a lot, I suppose.	
FENISA:	If you bring him to me, Tristan, a hundred ducats and the dress suit all are yours.	2625
TRISTAN:	Your feet I kiss.	
FENISA:	Goodbye.	
TRISTAN:	Goodbye.	
LUCINDO: [to Don Felix]	I tell you this is the reason for my distress.	
FENISA:	I'll be waiting for you, my honey.	2630
LUCINDO:	Bring the money and don't be late.	
FENISA:	And remember, love, that the rate is thirty percent for the money.	
LUCINDO:	Whatever you say.	
CELIA: [aside to Fenisa]	Who did you plan to ask for the money?	

FENISA: A mí;
que los dos mil tengo allí:
los mil haré que me den
sobre joyas y vestidos.
Treinta por ciento, ¿es ganancia
dime, de poca importancia?
Y éste pierde los sentidos
por mí, y si vende, es muy llano
que me ha de dar cuanto tenga.

CELIA: Guarda, señora, no venga
con intento más villano;
que los hombres suelen ser
astutos en la venganza.

FENISA: Al que dellos más alcanza
le engaña cualquier mujer.
Vamos por el Aduana,
y en el registro veré
su hacienda, para que esté
segura.

CELIA: Esa prenda es llana,
porque del libro sabrás,
y el registro, lo que trae.

Vanse los dos.

DON FÉLIX: Si en engaño no cae,
lindo gatazo le das.

LUCINDO: Que ella me le diese a mí
es lo que agora deseo.

DON FÉLIX: Que se va trazando creo
para que suceda así.

El capitán Osorio y Dinarda.

OSORIO: No hay para qué satisfacerme en nada;
yo sé que sois honrado caballero.

LUCINDO: Gente es ésta. Volved a la posada
mientras que solicito este dinero.
Y si habéis de matar por propia espada
ése que os ofendió, deciros quiero
más seguro camino.

DON FÉLIX: Yo quisiera
que con secreto mi venganza fuera.

[Vanse don Félix, Lucindo y los criados.]

DINARDA: Que estuviera Fenisa en mi aposento
no niego, Capitán; pero es muy llano

FENISA:	I'll ask me. I have two thousand, while I'll get the other thousand through pawning my dresses and my jewels. Thirty percent is just too good: I wouldn't pass it if I could. This fellow is the prince of fools; when he sells all his merchandise I'm sure he'll give me all he gets.	2635

2640 |
CELIA:	Don't be the smart one who forgets that a dumb yokel can be wise; when men take vengeance they can be much cleverer than you suppose.	2645
FENISA:	No matter how much a man knows he can't fool a woman like me. Let's go down to the Customs Shed and in the registry you can see what he has, and then our plan will be foolproof.	2650
CELIA:	It's as you've said: the registry book of the city will list everything that he's brought.	2655

[The two leave.]

FELIX:	If in your trap she isn't caught you'll be giving her a nice kitty.	
LUCINDO:	No; what will happen, I suspect, is that she will give one to me.	
FELIX:	And your strategy seems to be working out just as you expect.	2660

Captain Osorio and Dinarda

OSORIO:	I don't require satisfaction from you. You are an honored gentleman, I'm sure.	
LUCINDO:	Shh! There are people here. You go back to the inn; meanwhile, the money I'll procure. If you plan to take sword to that man who caused you such offense, please let me assure you, there is a better way.	2665
FELIX:	My strategy is to achieve my vengeance secretly.	

[Don Felix, Lucindo and the servants exit.]
Dinarda and Osorio

DINARDA:	That Fenisa was in my room is true, Captain; I won't deny it; but it's plain	2670

	que os vino a ver.	
Osorio:	Yo sé su pensamiento,	
	y sé también su proceder liviano.	
	Encarcelar al sol, prender el viento,	
	me pareció más fácil que el tirano	2675
	pecho desta mujer rendirse a un hombre,	
	si es cosa justa que mujer la nombre.	
	Con esto ha conservado el artificio	
	de pescar las haciendas extranjeras;	
	porque ese amor en gente de ese oficio	2680
	derriba por el suelo sus quimeras;	
	mas como el más espléndido edificio,	
	que inmortal a los tiempos consideras,	
	está sujeto al rayo, tú lo fuiste,	
	que con su libertad en tierra diste.	2685
	Ella te adora, yo lo sé: ¿qué dudas?	
Dinarda:	Y ¿oféndote, por dicha, en que me adore?	
Osorio:	Están las piedras, del milagro, mudas;	
	que lo es muy grande que te busque y llore.	
	Mas si a quien tantos desnudó desnudas,	2690
	no dudes que tu ingenio se mejore,	
	por haber engañado al mismo engaño,	
	al mismo enredo, astucia, traza y daño.	
	Corrido de las burlas que me ha hecho	
	y a tantos, al fin hombres, y extranjeros,	2695
	quiero que pruebes a vengar mi pecho,	
	solamente en materia de dineros.	
Dinarda:	Si para alguna cosa de provecho	
	fuere, don Juan, mi vida y sus aceros,	
	ordena, manda, corta, pon y quita;	2700
	que tú me obligas y un agravio incita.	
Osorio:	¿Agravio a ti?	
Dinarda:	Después sabrás el cuento.	
Osorio:	Mira: ninguna cosa estas mujeres	
	buscan ni intentan, más que el casamiento.	
	Toca esta tecla, si engañarlas quieres:	2705
	debe de ser la causa el escarmiento	
	de sus livianos gustos y placeres;	
	y cuando aquesto no les dé codicia,	
	el librarse también de la justicia.	
	Fuera desto, el temor que al tiempo tienen,	2710
	viendo que ya se acaba la hermosura,	
	y que si a verse con arrugas vienen,	
	no tienen cama o posesión segura.	
	Muchos verás que así las entretienen,	
	diciendo que hoy, mañana, y por ventura	2715

	she went there to see you.
Osorio:	I know her view
of men; I know she is fickle and vain.
If you ask me, it is easier to
put the sun in jail or hold back the rain
than for this woman to a man defer;
if woman is the proper name for her!
That's how she is an expert in the art
of fishing foreign purses from their banks;
you know those women, no matter how smart
they are, love knocks them down into the ranks
of fools. Like a splendid building, apart
from mortal things, safe from time's cruel pranks,
can nonetheless by lightning bolts be downed:
you knocked her freedom flat into the ground.
She loves you, I am sure: how can you doubt?
Dinarda:	Does it offend you that she fell for me?
Osorio:	It's so miraculous, the stones should shout,
to see her chasing you in misery.
But if you fleece the fleecer, you can flout
your cleverness in any company:
if you deceive that essence of deceit,
that fair conniver, trickster, thief and cheat.
I am so angry at what she has done
to me, to foreigners, the whole male race,
I want you to avenge me: you're the one
to take her money, put her in her place.
Dinarda:	If you can use the service of Don Juan,
his life and sword I offer for your case:
I'm yours to order, ask, guide or command.
She's wronged us both, and that shall guide my hand.
Osorio:	She wronged you?
Dinarda:	Later I'll tell you the story.
Osorio:	Listen, you know what women want from life,
you know that marriage is their only glory.
If you'd deceive them, hint what a good wife
they'd make you: that's the way to make them sorry;
That puts their fickle pleasures to the knife.
And if that doesn't whet their appetite,
the chance to get away with something might.
Another option is their fear of time,
seeing their beauty fade and disappear,
to them one wrinkle is a horrid crime
that steals their bed, possessions and career.
That's why so many men sing them a rhyme
about today, tomorrow and next year

Line numbers: 2675, 2680, 2685, 2690, 2695, 2700, 2705, 2710, 2715

	en algunos es flor. ¿Hasme entendido?	
Dinarda:	¿Tú quieres que me finja su marido?	
Osorio:	Déjame hacer; verás el fin que llevo.	

[Vanse.]
Dinarda y Osorio en casa de Fenisa

Dinarda:	Poco a poco a su casa hemos llegado.	
Osorio:	Tú serás de su Troya Sinón nuevo.	2720

[Salen Fenisa y Celia.]

Fenisa:	Todo el dinero tengo ya contado.	
Celia:	Paréceme, Fenisa, extraño cebo del anzuelo de amor tanto ducado.	
Fenisa:	¿No ves que me informé de los que tiene? Llámame al Capitán.	
Celia:	Él mismo viene.	2725
Fenisa: *[aparte al Capitán]*	A buscarte enviaba.	
Osorio:	¿En qué te sirvo?	
Fenisa:	Cierto dinero doy a cambio a un hombre, codiciosa de ver tanta ganancia; y porque espero otra mayor, querría que dijeses que es tuyo, y que es hacienda de unas doncellas.	2730
Osorio:	¿No te da resguardo?	
Fenisa:	Danme cincuenta cajas, por lo menos, de paños y de sedas de Valencia, y cien pipas de aceite registradas. Desto tendré las llaves y el seguro de las guardas del Rey; que sin mi orden no se dará a su dueño ni a otro alguno.	2735
Osorio:	Paréceme muy bien.	
Fenisa:	¿Cómo no llegas, don Juan?	
Osorio:	Porque está agora vergonzoso de cierta pretensión.	
Fenisa:	Malicias tuyas.	2740
Osorio:	¿Cómo malicias? ¡Vive Dios, que quise sabiendo que has estado en su aposento, pasarle el pecho con aquesta daga, y que me dijo que le perdonase,	

	and youth and flowers. Do you get my drift?	
DINARDA:	You'd have me offer marriage as a gift?	
OSORIO:	Let me fix things. Watch me dissimulate.	

[They exit.]
Dinarda and Osorio in a room in Fenisa's house

DINARDA:	We're here: I didn't see how fast we'd strolled.	
OSORIO:	You're Sinon of her Troy, and here's the gate.	2720

[Fenisa and Celia enter.]

FENISA:	I've counted every single piece of gold.	
CELIA:	These ducats seem to me a funny bait, Fenisa, for love's hook, if truth be told.	
FENISA:	I informed myself exactly of his holdings. Go call the Captain.	
CELIA:	There he is.	2725
FENISA: *[aside to the Captain]*	I sent for you.	
OSORIO:	How can I serve you now?	
FENISA:	I'm lending certain monies to a man who's eager for the profit he can make. And since I hope to garner more myself, you say the money's yours, from the estate of some young women.	2730
OSORIO:	Don't you hold a mortgage?	
FENISA:	He's given me some fifty trunks and crates of fine Valencian silks and other cloth, a hundred barrels of the finest oil. He's giving me the keys, and I have talked to the king's guards: they've promised me that they won't release the goods without my command.	2735
OSORIO:	That seems all right to me.	
FENISA:	Why don't you come join us, Don Juan?	
OSORIO:	The plans he has for you make him bashful.	
FENISA:	You're fooling me, I'm sure.	2740
OSORIO:	Me, fooling you! By God, I tell you when I found you'd been with him I tried to carve his heart out with this dagger that you see, and would have if he hadn't asked that I	

	porque si alguna cosa te había dicho,	2745
	era con sólo intento de casarse!	
	Yo, viendo la ocasión de tu remedio,	
	y que con él casada, si te lleva	
	a España, allá serás lo que quisieres,	
	quiero perder de mi derecho y gusto	2750
	porque te ganes tú; que por ventura	
	si voy a pretender como sospecho,	
	te acordarás que tu remedio he hecho.	
Fenisa:	¡Ay, Capitán! ¿Engáñasme?	
Osorio:	No creas	
	que en mi vida engañé mujer ninguna.	2755
Fenisa:	¡Ay, español, cómo conozco agora	
	la verdad española y el buen trato!	
	Si se efectúa, os doy el mismo día	
	dos cadenas que valgan mil ducados.	
Osorio:	Yo le he dicho a don Juan que estás muy rica.	2760
Fenisa:	No engañas a don Juan; porque si digo	
	verdad, puedo esta noche darle en dote	
	catorce mil ducados como uno.	

Tristán

Tristán:	Lucindo, mi señor, queda esperando	
	con los dos de la Aduana.	
Fenisa:	Osorio, vamos.	2765
	Tú, Celia, dile a Estacio y a Fabricio	
	carguen ese dinero y que me sigan.	
Osorio:	Despediréme de don Juan.	
Fenisa:	Pues dile	
	que es alma desta vida.	
Dinarda: [al Capitán]	¿Qué se ha hecho?	
Osorio:	A un negocio forzoso los dos vamos.	2770
	Está loca Fenisa, y me promete	
	mil ducados, don Juan, en dos cadenas...	
	Quédate por aquí.	
Dinarda:	Guárdete el cielo.	
Tristán: [aparte]	¡Oh, qué bien se concierta! Agora es tiempo,	
	Fortuna, de tu paso diligente.	2775
	¡Por Dios, que va a mamarla dulcemente!	

[*Vanse todos menos Dinarda.*]

| Dinarda: | Perdidos pasos doy, gastando al viento | |

	forgive him; for if he had talked with you	2745
	it was to ask you to become his wife!	
	I thought that way you might be reformed,	
	that if you married him and went to Spain	
	you could become there anything you liked.	
	My rights, and pleasures, I'll give up to him	2750
	so you can wed; for if, as I suspect,	
	my claim to loving you is over now	
	you'll know I've done you justice anyhow.	
FENISA:	Captain! Are you deceiving me?	
OSORIO:	Be sure	
	I've not deceived one woman in my life.	2755
FENISA:	Oh, my dear Spaniard! Now I know the truth	
	of all they tell of loving Spanish ways!	
	If this should come to pass, that day two chains	
	that cost a thousand ducats shall be yours.	
OSORIO:	I've told Don Juan that you are very rich.	2760
FENISA:	You don't deceive Don Juan; to tell the truth,	
	I could give him ten thousand ducats more	
	in dowry just as soon as give him one.	

[Tristan enters.]

TRISTAN:	My master, young Lucindo, waits for us	
	with the Customs men.	
FENISA:	Osorio, let's go.	2765
	You, Celia, tell Estacio and Fabricio	
	to take those money bags and follow me.	
OSORIO:	I'll tell Don Juan goodbye.	
FENISA:	Tell him as well	
	that he's my soul's life.	
DINARDA:		
[to the Captain]	What's happened now?	
OSORIO:	We two have urgent business to attend.	2770
	Fenisa's lost her head: she's promised me,	
	Don Juan, a thousand ducats in two chains....	
	Wait for us here.	
DINARDA:	I will. Now, go with God.	
TRISTAN:		
[aside]	How well the plan is working! Now's the time,	
	Dame Fortune, when you must cooperate.	2775
	By God, I think she's nibbling at the bait.	

[All but Dinarda exit.]

DINARDA:	I've lost my way, I vent into the air	

           suspiros, llantos, locas diligencias:
           ya no me queda en qué probar paciencias,
           que todo lo venció mi sufrimiento.   2780
              Si amor es un continuo pensamiento,
           ¿qué mucho que le rompan mil ausencias?
           Pues querer que me quieran por violencias,
           ni es ley de amor ni generoso intento.
              Mudóse Albano: ¡oh tiempos miserables!   2785
           Y ¡blasonan los hombres que adoramos,
           que sus firmezas son incontrastables!
              Mujeres sin disculpa nos mudamos;
           los hombres no, porque si son mudables,
           dicen que es por la causa que les damos.   2790

Albano

ALBANO: Mucho me huelgo de hallaros,
           don Juan, solo en este puesto.

DINARDA: Y yo de veros y hablaros;
           que también vengo dispuesto
           a informarme y a informaros.   2795

ALBANO:
[aparte]   ¡Válame Dios! ¿Que éste sea
           don Juan, y que no es Dinarda,
           quién ha de haber que lo crea?

DINARDA:
[aparte]   Mucho el temor me acobarda,
           que conocerme desea.   2800
              Pues téngolo de negar,
           si aquí supiese morir.
[alto]   Ya que me venís a hablar,
           o comenzad a decir,
           o comenzad a escuchar.   2805

ALBANO: Cuando en esta casa entrastes,
           sabíades mi intención:
           ¿por qué vos después llegastes?

DINARDA: Eso está en el corazón,
           que vos siempre me negastes.   2810
              Y sólo Dios lo sabría;
           porque un hombre al fin mudable,
           tendrá dos mil cada día.

ALBANO:
[aparte]   ¡Jesús! Que mire, que hable,
           es la misma prenda mía.   2815
              Pero Celia me ha contado
           que de Fenisa ha gozado,
           y esto no pudiera ser
           siendo este don Juan mujer,

  my wild complaints, mad weeping and laments.
  There's nowhere left to try my arguments,
  for all is lost to suffering and care.   2780
   If love leads to continuous despair,
  no wonder absence breeds impermanence.
  To force a man to love, with violence,
  is not emotion's way, not kind, nor fair.
   Albano's changed: oh age contemptible!   2785
  And even yet the men we worship claim
  their constancy is unassailable.
   We women change our feelings without shame;
  men find excuses: if they're culpable,
  it's that we make them so; we are to blame.   2790

[Albano enters.]

ALBANO: I am pleased to see you appear,
  Don Juan, alone as we agreed.

DINARDA: As I am glad to find you here;
  for I too come ready to heed
  your words: both to speak and to hear.   2795

ALBANO:
[aside]   God help me! This is Don Juan? It
  seems more like Dinarda to me.
  I don't believe it, not one bit.

DINARDA:
[aside]   I'm frightened to death, I admit.
  What if he seeks my company?   2800
   I can't let him see me this way.
  How I wish I could disappear.
[aloud]   You've come to talk to me, I fear:
  so say then what you have to say,
  or else hear what you have to hear.   2805

ALBANO: If when you came to this house you
  knew what my intentions were, where-
  fore did you seek this interview?

DINARDA: The heart can give reasons to spare,
  that heart you never let me share;   2810
   the reason I have come, God knows.
  Besides, you fickle men dispose
  of two thousand hearts every day.

ALBANO:
[aside]   Christ! I look, and my eyes disclose
  the girl from whom I sailed away.   2815
   Yet Celia's informed me how he
  has taken Fenisa to bed,
  and I don't know how that can be,
  if Don Juan's a woman instead,

	como lo tengo soñado.	2820
	Quíerome disimular.	
[alto]	Vuestros criados hablé	
	cuando me quise informar.	
Dinarda:	Pues bien, ¿a qué efecto fue?	
Albano:	A efecto de preguntar	2825
	vuestra patria y vuestro nombre;	
	y burláronse de mí.	
Dinarda:	Son pajes.	
Albano:	No porque asombre	
	el veros venir aquí	
	tan gallardo y gentilhombre,	2830
	que deso no estoy celoso;	
	más para sólo saber	
	si sois hombre generoso,	
	porque con esta mujer	
	procedáis más cauteloso.	2835
Dinarda:	¡Qué gracia en eso tenéis!	
	¿De cautelas me advertís?	
	Sin duda que las sabéis?	
Albano:	Vos, ¿para qué la servís?	
Dinarda:	Vos, ¿para qué la queréis?	2840
Albano:	Yo por sólo entretener	
	la ausencia de una mujer	
	de quien desdichas me apartan,	
	que eternamente se hartan	
	de verme morir y arder.	2845
Dinarda:	¿Vos queréis mujer ausente?	
Albano:	Quiero una mujer que adoro,	
	tan bella, que no consiente	
	que se le compare el oro,	
	ni el mismo sol en Oriente.	2850
	Como a imagen la tenía	
	en el altar del respeto,	
	donde el alma le ofrecía;	
	cuyo retrato os prometo	
	hace en vos la ausencia mía.	2855
	Y de colores de amor	
	en la tabla del deseo	
	os hizo con tal primor,	
	que parece que la veo,	
	aunque la cubre el temor.	2860
Dinarda:	Quisiera saber quién era	
	para escribirle ese engaño	

FENISA'S HOOK, OR FENISA THE HOOKER

	which is what she appears to me.	2820
	What I know I had better hide.	
[aloud]	I asked your servants to have my curiosity satisfied.	
DINARDA:	What did you want to clarify?	
ALBANO:	I requested that they provide me with your nationality and name; and then they laughed at me.	2825
DINARDA:	Just like pages!	
ALBANO:	I did not find it strange to see you here enshrined with such grace, and gentility. I am not envious of that; but I did think it necessary to discover if you are very generous; then the caveat is with this one you must be wary.	2830 2835
DINARDA:	If I'm careful, then where's the sport? If caution is what you implore, then you must be the cautious sort.	
ALBANO:	You, tell me why you pay her court.	
DINARDA:	You, tell me what you want her for.	2840
ALBANO:	I want her just to occupy me while misfortunes absent me from the woman who makes me sigh; misfortunes that eternally tire of watching me burn and die.	2845
DINARDA:	You love a woman far away?	
ALBANO:	I love the woman I adore: so lovely gold cannot convey her brilliance; as competitor the morning sun cannot hold sway. I hold her image in my mind on the altar of my respect, with my soul's offering enshrined; yet my absence makes me detect your portrait with hers intertwined. And with love's most beautiful hues, mixed on the palate of desire, it painted you with such a muse that her face in yours I admire, even though fear your smile subdues.	2850 2855 2860
DINARDA:	I would like to find out her name to write to her the way you cheat	

	que vuestra fe vitupera,	
	porque viendo el desengaño,	
	ausente os aborreciera.	2865
	Que a una piedra mueve a risa	
	que aquí finjáis adorar	
	a quien vuestro olvido pisa,	
	y me vengáis a matar	
	por los celos de Fenisa.	2870
	Pues, Albano, estad atento	
	a lo que os voy a decir	
	de este antiguo pensamiento…	
	ni tengo que competir,	
	ni vuestros engaños siento.	2875
	Deste que agora tenéis,	
	os digo que no intentéis	
	entrar desde hoy en su casa,	
	porque Fenisa se casa.	
ALBANO:	¿Con quién?	
DINARDA:	Allá lo sabréis.	2880
	Y ¿qué sirve preguntar	
	con quién se casa esta dama?	
	Amando en otro lugar,	
	¿no veis que en eso se infama	
	la que estaba en el altar?	2885
ALBANO:	Oíd.	
DINARDA:	¿Yo cuentos ajenos?	
ALBANO: *[aparte]* *[alto]*	¡Ay, ojos de engaños llenos! ¿Con quién se casa?	
DINARDA:	Conmigo.	
ALBANO:	¿Con vos?	
DINARDA:	Sí, conmigo digo.	
ALBANO:	Por muchos años y buenos.	2890
[Vase Dinarda.]		
ALBANO:	Acabóse. Ya, ¿qué intento?	
	¡Por Dios, que me vuelve loco	
	tan extraño pensamiento!	
	Ya mi desengaño toco,	
	ya con la verdad consiento;	2895
	ya me parece que es ella,	
	ya me parece que no;	
	mas lo que saco de vella	
	es que en mí resucitó	
	cuanto he pasado por ella.	2900

	on your faithfulness, to your shame;	
	so when she sees through your deceit,	
	absent she can hold you to blame.	2865
	It would bring laughter to a stone	
	to see how your love is so zealous	
	for the woman you left alone;	
	yet you'd kill me because you're jealous	
	of Fenisa in every bone.	2870
	Albano, listen closely to	
	the words I'm going to repeat	
	about the things you said you'd do:	
	there's no cause for me to compete,	
	nor am I hurt by your deceit.	2875
	There's one thing I want to make clear	
	about our Fenisa: I say	
	from now on you shall not go near	
	her house, because she weds today.	
ALBANO:	Whom does she marry?	
DINARDA:	Soon you'll hear.	2880
	What good is it for you to search	
	to find out her new husband's name?	
	Since you love elsewhere, you besmirch	
	another's honor. You defame	
	the one left waiting in the church.	2885
ALBANO:	Listen.	
DINARDA:	Spare me your history.	
ALBANO: *[aside]* *[aloud]*	How deceit makes bitter tears run. Tell me whom she's marrying.	
DINARDA:	Me.	
ALBANO:	You?	
DINARDA:	I assure you I'm the one.	
ALBANO:	May you live long and happily.	2890
[Dinarda exits.]		
ALBANO:	There, she's gone. Now what shall I do?	
	By God, these crazy thoughts of mine	
	are driving me insane anew!	
	First deceit draws its strange design	
	and then the truth falls into line.	2895
	Sometimes I think I see her there,	
	Sometimes I think it can't be her.	
	But there's one thing I can infer	
	from seeing her again: I care	
	for her just as before, I swear.	2900

[Vase.]
Camilo y Albano, en la calle

CAMILO: En vuestra busca he venido
por la ciudad descompuesto,
y a gran ventura he tenido
hallaros en este puesto.

ALBANO: Quedo, Camilo. ¿Qué ha sido? 2905

CAMILO: Un hombre medio embozado,
y español recién llegado,
solícito preguntaba
adónde Albano posaba,
entre uno y otro soldado. 2910
    Llegué y díjeselo, y luego
le pregunté qué os quería.
Mostró algún desasosiego,
y dijo que volvería,
sin que bastase mi ruego. 2915
    Seguíle, y en su posada
pregunté quién era.

ALBANO: ¿Y bien?

CAMILO: Ninguno me dijo nada.
Fui a la mar, que fue también
una advertencia extremada, 2920
    y una nave valenciana
hallé que había surgido,
pienso que ayer de mañana,
y que aquésta había traído
cierta gente sevillana. 2925

ALBANO: ¿Sevillana dijo?

CAMILO: Sí,
pues don Félix está aquí,
el hermano de Dinarda,
de alguna traición te guarda.

[Hablan bajo.]
Lucindo y Tristán

LUCINDO: Altamente la cogí. 2930

TRISTÁN: Divinamente cayó.

LUCINDO: ¿Está en la nave el dinero?

TRISTÁN: Nuestra gente le embarcó.

LUCINDO: Pues si hace viento, ¿qué espero?

TRISTÁN: Lo mismo te digo yo. 2935
    Ésta tiene mil valientes,
que, descubierto el engaño,

[He exits.]
Camilo and Albano, in the street

CAMILO:
    I've been wandering all day long
    looking for you; I'm so upset;
    and you have been here all along.
    How lucky that at last we've met.

ALBANO: Calm yourself, Camilo: what's wrong?   2905

CAMILO:
    A man half covered by a cloak,
    a Spaniard who's just come ashore
    is asking all the soldier folk
    where Albano lives; he asked for
    you with every sentence he spoke.   2910
      So I went and told him, and when
    I asked him his business with you
    he got all upset, which was when
    he said he had something to do
    now but would hurry back again.   2915
      I followed him, and at his inn
    I asked who he was.

ALBANO: And they said...?

CAMILO:
    Nothing. Not one man would begin.
    So I went to the port instead,
    where I found a ship had come in   2920
      from Valencia, I heard them say.
    I'm certain it was not until
    yesterday before noon that they
    reached shore and that the ship was filled
    with certain people from Seville.   2925

ALBANO: You say they are from Seville?

CAMILO: Yes.
    And since Don Felix is here (he
    is Dinarda's brother), I press
    you: guard yourself from treachery.

[*They speak softly.*]
Lucindo and Tristan

LUCINDO: I caught her nicely, I confess.   2930

TRISTAN: You really gave her her reward!

LUCINDO: Is all the money on the boat?

TRISTAN: Our people loaded it on board.

LUCINDO: The wind is up; let's get afloat.

TRISTAN:
    I am completely in accord.   2935
      She owns a thousand ruffians
    and when they all find out about

	importa hallarnos ausentes.	
Lucindo:	¡Quién se hallara al desengaño!	
Tristán:	Ni lo digas ni lo intentes.	2940
	Conozco que fuera justo	
	alquilar una ventana	
	para mirar con tal gusto	
	esta Circe cortesana	
	rabiar de puro disgusto;	2945
	pero, el peligro advertido	
	cójanos en alta mar,	
	Lucindo, aqueste rüído.	
Lucindo:	Tristán, ¡cuál ha de quedar!	
Tristán:	Notable gatazo ha sido.	2950
	Todos tenemos anzuelo.	
	¡Hola, pícara gallarda!	
	Quédate adiós.	
Lucindo: *[reparando en Albano y Camilo]*	¡Qué recelo me ha dado esta gente!	
Tristán:	Aguarda. No es nada.	
Lucindo:	Dad viento, cielo,	2955
	a la nave con que trato;	
	que de fama y tiempo ingrato	
	mayor opinión espero,	
	que Jasón por su cordero,	
	por este notable gato.	2960
	Cese la famosa historia	
	del vellocino que frisa	
	con la más alta memoria;	
	que el anzuelo de Fenisa	
	me ha dado mayor victoria.	2965

[Vase.]
Tristán; Albano y Camilo, *retirados*

Tristán:	¡Cielos, dad viento a la nave	
	en que me vuelvo a Valencia,	
	para que en ella me alabe	
	que pude vencer la ciencia	
	de la mujer que más sabe!	2970
	Cien ducados y un vestido	
	hoy a Fenisa he cogido;	
	mi amo tres mil ducados,	
	que, los dos mil rescatados,	
	mil por la ganancia han sido.	2975

	us, we should be in foreign lands.	
LUCINDO:	I'd like to watch when they find out.	
TRISTAN:	Don't try, don't think it, don't make plans.	2940
	I know that what we'd like to do	
	is rent ourselves a window box	
	so that we can enjoy the view	
	of this Circe courtesan fox	
	getting so angry she turns blue.	2945
	If we know the danger, let's heed	
	it: when we hear the noise we need	
	to be a long way out at sea.	
LUCINDO:	Tristan, just think how she will be.	
TRISTAN:	You've played her a fine one indeed.	2950
	Everybody has his own hook.	
	Hello, my lovely picaroon,	
	and goodbye!	
LUCINDO: *[noticing Albano and Camilo]*	I don't like the look these people give me.	
TRISTAN:	Don't get shook, it's nothing.	
LUCINDO:	Winds, be opportune	2955
	and blow hard for this ship of mine.	
	Ungrateful time and fame's caprice	
	my deeds will render more divine	
	than Jason and his golden fleece,	
	for this deceitful masterpiece.	2960
	That famous lamb, no matter how	
	often found in history's book,	
	has met its match in glory now,	
	for my triumph Fenisa's hook	
	with unceasing fame will endow.	2965

[They exit.]
Tristan; Albano and Camilo, in the background

TRISTAN:	Oh winds, be opportune and blow	
	me to Valencia right away	
	so everyone back there can say	
	though she knew all there was to know,	
	her science I could overthrow.	2970
	A hundred ducats and a suit	
	is what Fenisa lost to me;	
	my master got a lot more loot:	
	three thousand, with the two that he	
	gave her leaves him one thousand free.	2975

Quédate en paz, pescadora
de bolsas, anzuelo extraño
de gatos, áspid que llora:
mamaste tu mismo engaño,
Circe de enredos autora. 2980
    Ya no será de importancia
poner cebo a la ganancia,
llorar, mover y fingir;
que ojos que nos vieren ir,
no nos verán más en Francia. 2985

[Vase.]

CAMILO: Bien me parece, y sería
cuerda cosa ir a la mar.

ALBANO: De esa nave en que venía
me quiero luego informar
antes que se cierre el día; 2990
    que no faltará algún hombre
que sepa también el nombre,
y las señas me drían.

CAMILO: Agravios, ¿qué no podrán?
Lo que intenta, no te asombre, 2995
    porque escribe el ofendido
en mármol, y el que ofendió
en agua.

ALBANO: Pues he sabido
que viene, no seré yo
quien viva con tanto olvido. 3000

CAMILO: Bien haces, porque en efeto,
el que agravia, ni de un muro
ni del lugar más secreto,
aun no ha de vivir seguro
de sí mismo, si es discreto. 3005

[Vanse.]
Fenisa y Celia

CELIA: Contenta vienes.

FENISA: No estuve
en mi vida más contenta.
La suerte, a mi bien atenta,
sobre su rueda me sube.
    He vuelto un hombre a mi casa 3010
que la puede enriquecer;
y seré de otro mujer,
que por lo menos me abrasa.

CELIA: Seguro queda el dinero

	Rest in peace, you angler of purses,	
	you pocket picking whiz with hooks,	
	you wasp that stinging tears disburses;	
	you've crooked yourself, you queen of crooks,	
	you Circe, cursed with your own curses.	2980
	No uses for your bait remain.	
	Now you've no reason left to feign	
	weeping, to posture, or betray;	
	the eyes that watch us sail away	
	will never see us here again.	2985

[He exits.]
Albano and Camilo

CAMILO: In my opinion, it would be
a good thing to put out to sea.

ALBANO: All right, but I'm anxious to find
out about the ship in which he
came, before this day's left behind. 2990
 There has to be someone around
who this fellow's name can recall,
and tell me where he can be found.

CAMILO: For insult's sake, all things befall.
His eagerness should not astound 2995
 you, for the insulted engraves
on marble; the insulter writes
on water.

ALBANO: Since he's here, by rights
I must find him. No one behaves
with honor if this chance he waives. 3000

CAMILO: You're doing right, for in effect
the one who insults should not live
in safety: although he selects
the highest, thickest walls to give
him peace, he should be circumspect. 3005

[They exit.]
Fenisa and Celia

CELIA: How satisfied you look.

FENISA: I feel
just as happy as I can be:
good fortune's looking out for me.
Watch her lift me up on her wheel!
 I've brought one man into my life 3010
who'll enrich me at every turn;
while with another's fire I burn,
and that man will make me his wife....

CELIA: I'm sure the money that you gave

	que a Lucindo agora has dado.	3015
FENISA:	¡Con qué astucia le he engañado!	
	él es lindo majadero.	
	¿Hay hombre tan mentecato?	
	¿Estas bestias cría España?	
CELIA:	Es toda España montaña	3020
	bárbara en ingenio y trato.	
	¡Mira tú qué policía,	
	pues de plata que le ofrece	
	la India, a Italia enriquece,	
	a Francia y a Berbería!	3025
	¿Qué nación sustenta el mundo	
	donde no corra por ley	
	plata y armas de su rey?	
FENISA:	¡Qué bien mis negocios fundo!	
	Treinta por ciento; y tras esto,	3030
	lo que queda que pescar.	
	Déstos querría yo hallar.	
CELIA:	Pocos hallarás tan presto.	
FENISA:	Las llaves del almacén	
	he puesto en el escritorio.	3035
	¿Adónde, Celia, fue Osorio?	
CELIA:	Fue por don Juan.	
FENISA:	¡Ay, mi bien!	

Bernardo

BERNARDO:	Déme vuestra señoría,	
	como a su paje, la mano.	
FENISA:	¡Amigo Bernardo, hermano!...	3040
BERNARDO:	Goces de tal compañía	
	más de mil años, amén.	
FENISA:	Toma este anillo, Bernardo,	
	por el español gallardo	
	que es dueño tuyo y mi bien.	3045
	Mira que el diamante vale	
	cuarenta escudos y más.	
BERNARDO:	Cuando me mandes, verás	
	que hay quien su firmeza iguale.	

Fabio

FABIO:	Della vostra signoria	3050
	bacio le mani e li piedi,	
	e voglio chieder mercedi.	
FENISA:	¡Oh, Fabio!	

	Lucindo now is quite secure.	3015
FENISA:	How cleverly I did conjure it. Isn't he a stupid knave! How could he be so dumb? Is that the sort of beast they raise in Spain?	
CELIA:	There's not one man on hill or plain who's not as stupid as a bat! Look what a fine sense of finance: for all the silver ducats which the Indies give to her enrich Italy, Barbary and France! What nation in this world has got ahead without the potent charms of its silver and royal arms?	3020

3025 |
FENISA:	What a good business sense I've got! Thirty percent; and in addition, all he's got left for me to fish. Some more like him is what I'd wish!	3030
CELIA:	Few come so quickly to perdition.	
FENISA:	The warehouse keys I've laid out on my desk there in the studio. Where, Celia, did Osorio go?	3035
CELIA:	For Don Juan.	
FENISA:	Oh, my love, Don Juan!	

[Bernardo enters.]

BERNARDO:	My ladyship, give me your hand. I'm yours, on that you can depend.	
FENISA:	My brother! Bernardo, my friend!...	3040
BERNARDO:	May such friends be at your command for the next hundred years: amen.	
FENISA:	Bernardo, take this ring of mine for that fair Spaniard, your divine lord and my handsomest of men. The diamond I estimate worth forty ducats anyhow.	3045
BERNARDO:	If you command me you'll see how his steadfastness I imitate.	

[Fabio enters.]

FABIO:	*Della vostra signoría bacio le mani,* and request *che con mercedi* I be blessed.	3050
FENISA:	Oh, Fabio.	

Fabio:	¡Oh, padrona mía!	
	Un secolo e più, signora,	
	godiate il vostro consorte,	3055
	contenta sin a la morte,	
	e dopo de morta ancora.	
	Mai abbiate gelosia,	
	e Dio vi done figliuoli,	
	maschi, belli et ispagnuoli.	3060
Fenisa:	El cielo hacerlo podría.	
	Toma esta joya, mi Fabio;	
	que esa lengua me consuela.	
Fabio:	¡Oh padroncina mia bella!	
Fenisa:	¡Oh paje discreto y sabio!	3065

Osorio

Osorio:	A decirte que le esperes	
	me envía el señor don Juan.	
Fenisa:	¡Oh famoso Capitán,	
	que mi padre y dueño eres!	
	Esta vuelta de cadena	3070
	en mi nombre has de traer.	
Osorio:	No era menester prender	
	a quien tu amor encadena;	
	mas ya que tan liberal	
	el cielo te fabricó,	3075
	traeréla en tu nombre yo,	
	a un esclavo tuyo igual.	
	Esto es gran favor, es mucho.	
Fabio:	¡Vedete che ca me doglio!	
	Non lo voglio, non lo voglio;	3080
	ma intratemelo in capuccio.	

Dinarda

Dinarda:	Perdona si me he tardado.	
Fenisa:	Seas, mi bien, bien venido.	
Dinarda:	Quien viene a ser tu marido,	
	al mayor bien ha llegado.	3085
Fenisa:	¿Qué te podría yo dar	
	por esa palabra, amores?	
Dinarda:	Muchas perlas, muchas flores	
	desa boca y dese azar.	
Fenisa:	Toma este rico diamante	3090
	para señal de mi fe.	
Dinarda:	Pues señal de prisión fue,	

FABIO:	*Oh, padrona mía.*	
	Un secolo e piú, signora,	
	godiate il vostro consorte,	3055
	contenta sin a la morte,	
	e dopo de morta ancora.	
	Mai abbiate gelosia,	
	e Dio vi done figliuoli,	
	maschi, belli et ispagnuoli.	3060
FENISA:	May the heavens bless your idea.	
	Come, Fabio, take this jewel, please.	
	Hearing that language is so fine.	
FABIO:	Oh, sweet *padroncina* of mine.	
FENISA:	Oh, page of rare abilities.	3065

[Osorio enters.]

OSORIO:	Don Juan has sent me here to tell	
	you to be sure await him here.	
FENISA:	Oh Captain, you grand cavalier,	
	you're my father and lord as well!	
	I want you to wear this length of	3070
	chain always henceforth in my name.	
OSORIO:	There was no need to lay this claim	
	on someone enchained by your love.	
	However, since the Heavens made	
	your character so generous,	3075
	it shall be by this amorous	
	servant of yours always displayed.	
	It's too much; you shouldn't have done it.	
FABIO:	Look at the way this puppy barks.	
	Non lo voglio's what he remarks,	3080
	then "please attach it to my bonnet."	

[Dinarda enters.]

DINARDA:	Forgive me if I've arrived late.	
FENISA:	You're welcome whenever you come.	
DINARDA:	And whoever comes to become	
	your husband's truly fortunate.	3085
FENISA:	What will you let me give to you	
	for that wonderful word, my love?	
DINARDA:	Give me all of the pearls, all of	
	the flowers that your lips bestrew.	
FENISA:	Take this rich diamond, it will be	3090
	of my constancy a portent.	
DINARDA:	As token of imprisonment,	

	sea él grillo y yo el amante.	
Fenisa:	En cambio de un gran palacio	
	hoy te da el alma Fenisa.	3095
Fabio:		
[aparte]	¡Por Dios, que reparte aprisa	
	lo que ha pescado despacio!	

Albano y Camilo

Albano:	Después de que por mil años	
	goces, hermosa Fenisa,	
	al señor don Juan de Lara,	3100
	honra y valor de Sevilla,	
	sabe que llegando al mar	
	para saber si venía	
	cierto don Félix, por quien	
	traigo en peligro la vida,	3105
	vi una nave valenciana	
	que con su zaloma y grita	
	izaba las blancas velas,	
	que ya el manso viento hería,	
	y que un hombre en una barca,	3110
	abordándola, decía:	
	"Albano, Albano, esa carta	
	daréis mañana a Fenisa."	
	En esto, un hombre en la playa	
	que a mi lado la tenía,	3115
	me la dio, y volviendo el rostro	
	a la nave que se iba,	
	dije: "Yo se la daré."	
	Y entonces, con mucha risa,	
	él y un amigo o criado	3120
	suben por el borde arriba.	
	La nave, izando el trinquete,	
	se alejó de las orillas,	
	porque el viento refrescaba,	
	hasta perderse de vista.	3125
	Yo no aguardé, cuidadoso	
	de saber lo que sería,	
	a mañana: esta es la carta.	

Fenisa:		
[aparte]	La color tengo perdida.	
[alto]	Abre, Osorio.	
Osorio:	Dice ansí:	3130
[lee]	"Si bien te acuerdas, arpía,	
	con artificioso anzuelo,	
	luto y lágrimas fingidas,	
	dos mil ducados pescaste..."	

	it shall be as leg irons to me.	
FENISA:	Love, if my soul is what you wish, there in your great palace it's yours.	3095
FABIO: [aside]	My God, what quick expenditures of what it took so long to fish.	

Albano and Camilo

ALBANO:	When you've snuggled tight, Fenisa for another thousand years with my lord Don Juan de Lara, strength and honor of Seville, you should know that when I went down to the shoreline of the sea to discern if one Don Felix, who's my mortal enemy, had come, I saw a boat sail for Valencia from the beach. Men were shouting, lines were flapping, sails were filling in the breeze, and one man, climbing aboard her from a skiff, shouted to me: "Hey, Albano, give this letter to Fenisa, I beseech." And with that another man there on the shore handed to me a note, and I turned as the ship was heading out to sea, and shouted: "I'll give it to her." Then with much hilarity this man, with friend or servant, climbed aboard and disappeared. So the ship hoisted its anchor, and sailed off out toward the deeps where the wind picked up, and soon the boat could no longer be seen. I was so anxious to find out what this business all could mean, that I ran here. Take the letter.	3100 3105 3110 3115 3120 3125
FENISA: [aside] [aloud]	I grow pale at what I hear. Read it out, Osorio.	
OSORIO:	All right: "Harpy: jog your memory how with artfully baited hook of mourning clothes and lying tears you fished up two thousand ducats…"	3130

FENISA: ¡Ah, Lucindo!

DINARDA: ¿Qué suspiras? 3135

FENISA: ¡Válgame Dios! ¿Qué es aquesto?

OSORIO:
[lee]
"Mas la industria, vengativa,
supo cobrar su dinero."

FENISA: ¿Cómo?

OSORIO:
[lee]
      "Una caja tenía,
para poder engañarte, 3140
seis varas de paño encima.
Las pipas todas son agua,
porque la primera pipa
tiene diez libras de aceite;
no harás poco si te labras. 3145
Tres mil ducados me diste;
no es mucho que mil que quedan
por este cambio me sirvan;
que si tú a treinta por ciento 3150
de tu ganancia querías,
de mentiras cobrarás,
pues has vendido mentiras."

FENISA: No leas; que si supiera
volar, o hubiera en Sicilia 3155
encantadores...

ALBANO: Detente.

FENISA: Déjame.

CAMILO: En vano porfías.
Ya la nave en alta mar,
todas las velas tendidas,
camina con viento en popa. 3160

FENISA: ¡Santo Dios!

CAMILO: ¿Qué te santiguas?

FENISA: Soy mujer; no os espantéis
que esto piense y que esto diga.
Perdona, amado don Juan;
que para la hacienda mía 3165
no importan tres mil ducados.

DINARDA: Mi bien, como no te aflijas,
yo no tengo mucha pena.

Don Félix y Donato, embozados; dos soldados

Fenisa:	Oh, Lucindo!	
Dinarda:	Do you weep?	3135
Fenisa:	God assist me; this is awful.	
Osorio: [reads]	"But vengeful ingenuity knew how to get the money."	
Fenisa:	What?	
Osorio: [reading]	"Those boxes were the key to pulling wool over your eyes. Cloth? There was just one piece. The kegs are all filled with water; though the first one, cleverly, has ten gallons of fine oil to deceive you gallantly. Two thousand ducats I gave you for three thousand you gave me; and that thousand profit will serve me well as I take my leave. If you wanted thirty percent return on that thieving deal, you'll get thirty percent in lies for investing such deceit."	3140 3145 3150
Fenisa:	Stop, stop. If I could fly away from here.... If in Sicily there were enchanters...	3155
Albano:	Say no more.	
Fenisa:	Let me be.	
Albano:	It's no use, I fear. The sails are set; the wind at stern has blown them far out to sea by now. He is gone.	
Fenisa:	Oh, my God!	3160
Camilo:	You cross yourself: what does that mean?	
Fenisa:	I'm a woman. Are you surprised to hear me say what I feel? Forgive me, my dearest Don Juan, if three thousand ducats seem little to one who has so much.	3165
Dinarda:	If you're not going to weep, my love, then I won't get upset.	

Don Felix and Donato, with their faces covered; two soldiers

Don Félix:	Siguiendo a los dos venía, y en esta casa se entraron.	3170
Soldado 1:	Aquí hay gente.	
Don Félix: [a Donato]	Aquí te arrima.	
Celia:	En la boda hay embozados.	
Don Félix:	Vuesas mercedes prosigan; que todo es gente de paz.	
Albano:	Antes parece enemiga. Desembócense, o ¡por Dios, que los eche con más prisa que entraron!	3175
Don Félix: [Desembózase]	Un hombre soy que he venido hasta Sicilia en busca vuestra.	
Albano:	¿Es don Félix?	3180
Don Félix:	Y sin traición os quería hablar en el campo a solas.	
Camilo:	Este es campo.	
Osorio:	Ya me obligan...	
Dinarda:	Ténganse, que estoy en medio. Díganme la causa, y dicha, yo los pondré en la campaña.	3185
Albano:	Don Félix tuvo en Sevilla una cuestión, de la cual sacó dos o tres heridas.	
Osorio:	¿No es más?	
Albano:	Si es más, no lo sé; él, que lo sabe, él lo diga.	3190
Don Félix:	Aunque es verdad que en los pechos me pusistes aquel día la pala, que no es agravio tengo por cuarenta firmas. No vengo por esa parte: más pesa la ofensa mía; que con la espada en la mano no hay hombre que agravios pida. Yo lo cobré con reñir; si me hirieron, fue desdicha, porque llegó vuestra espada como pudiera la mía.	3195 3200

FELIX:	I followed them down this street	
	and saw both go into that house.	3170
FIRST SOLDIER:	I hear people.	
FELIX:		
[to Donato]	Come back here.	
CELIA:	Hiding their faces? Something's wrong.	
FELIX:	Go on, gentlemen, feel free.	
	We are all peace-loving men.	
ALBANO:	Yet you look like enemies.	3175
	Show us your faces, or by God	
	I'll toss you out on the street	
	quicker than you came in.	
FELIX:	I'm
	a man	
[He uncovers.]	come to Sicily	
	in search of you.	
ALBANO:	Are you Don Felix?	3180
FELIX:	I want, without treachery,	
	in open field to have it out.	
CAMILO:	This field's open...	
OSORIO:	You force me...	
DINARDA:	Hold: you've caught me in the middle.	
	You explain what all this means	3185
	and I'll say whether you should fight.	
ALBANO:	Once Don Felix, in Seville,	
	was in an argument, from which	
	some trifling wounds he received.	
OSORIO:	It's not more than that?	
ALBANO:	I don't know.	3190
	But he knows all: let him speak.	
FELIX:	It's true that day you laid your hand	
	on me, but I did not feel	
	injured, and I have forty men	
	who'll swear that I'm not aggrieved.	3195
	That's not the reason I have come.	
	The offense weighs worse on me,	
	for no man can be affronted	
	once his sword has been unsheathed.	
	The fighting cleared my honor: it	3200
	was bad luck they wounded me.	
	Your sword achieved exactly what	
	my own could have achieved.	

Albano:	Pues ¿qué pedís?
Don Félix:	A mi hermana;
	y sin ella o sin la vida 3205
	de quien me la trujo aquí,
	no he de volver a Sevilla.
Albano:	Yo no tengo vuestra hermana.
Dinarda:	Si la enemistad antigua
	cesa, y las manos os dais, 3210
	y por esposa la estima
	Albano, como es razón,
	yo haré que venga ella misma
	a confirmar estas paces.
Don Félix:	Ésta es mi mano.
Albano:	Y la mía. 3215
Dinarda:	Pues sabed que soy Dinarda.
Fenisa:	¡Don Juan! ¡Mi esposo!
Albano:	Desvía;
	que mi mujer no es tu esposo.
Fenisa:	¡Don Juan!
Dinarda:	¿Qué don Juan, Fenisa?
	Mujer soy.
Fenisa:	Pues, Capitán, 3220
	será razón y justicia
	que me vuelvan lo que he dado.
	Dame mi cadena.
Osorio:	Mira
	si hay algún bravo que venga,
	y en el campo me la pida. 3225
Fenisa:	Bernardo, dame el diamante.
Bernardo:	¿Qué diamante?
Fenisa:	Tú, enemiga,
	dame el que te di.
Dinarda:	No creo
	que tú tengas cosa fina.
Fenisa:	Fabio, vuélveme la joya. 3230
Fabio:	Vattene in forca e t'impicca.
Camilo:	Aquí se acaba, senado,
	El anzuelo de Fenisa.

ALBANO:	What are you asking, then?	
FELIX:	My sister, and I swear that when I leave I'll either take her, or the life of the one who brought her here.	3205
ALBANO:	But I have no sister of yours.	
DINARDA:	If this ancient enmity ceases, and you two will shake hands, and as wife you will esteem her, Albano, as is your duty, I will celebrate this peace treaty by showing her to you.	3210
FELIX:	Here's my hand.	
ALBANO:	My hand is here.	3215
DINARDA:	Know that Dinarda is myself!	
FENISA:	Don Juan! My husband!	
ALBANO:	Let her be, for my bride can't be your husband.	
FENISA:	My Don Juan!	
DINARDA:	What Don Juan? See, Fenisa, I'm a woman.	
FENISA:	Well, then, justice and honesty demand, Captain, that you return my chain to me.	3220
OSORIO:	If there be a man who's brave enough to try, let him win the chain from me!	3225
FENISA:	Bernardo, give me my diamond.	
BERNARDO:	What diamond?	
FENISA:	What treachery! Give me my gift back.	
DINARDA:	That you'd have something that fine I can't believe.	
FENISA:	Fabio, give me back my jewels.	3230
FABIO:	*T'impicca* with your own pic.	
CAMILO:	Good friends, the hooker's hooked; and now **Fenisa's hook** is complete.	

About the translator:

David Gitlitz is the author of *La estructura lírica de la comedia de Lope de Vega* and numerous articles on Spanish Golden Age poetry, prose, and theater. His *Songs of Love and Death and In Between* is the most extensive translation of the poetry of Francisco de Quevedo into English, and his translation of *Guárdate de la agua mansa (Beware of Still Waters)* has been called by one reviewer "without a doubt the most admirable translation of a Spanish Golden Age play that I have ever encountered" (*Hispania*, 1985). He received a special award for translation of *Beware of Still Waters* at the Chamizal Festival of Golden Age theater in 1981.

A graduate of Oberlin College and Harvard University, Gitlitz has taught at Indiana University, the University of Nebraska, and at SUNY-Binghamton, where he is Dean of Harpur College and the College of Arts & Sciences.

In 1974, 1979, and 1987 Gitlitz led groups of student pilgrims on foot from southern France to Santiago de Compostela, winning in one year the National Council of Summer Sessions award for creative programming.

Trinity University Press acknowledges with appreciation that Professor Gitlitz submitted the manuscript to the publisher on disks. Through a cooperative effort among translator, publisher, and printer, the project was edited and processed onto the printer's system, using those disks.

The printer is Best Printing Company, Inc., Austin, Texas
The typeface is Goudy Oldstyle
The book design is in collaboration with Jerry Tokola
The art work is by Sandra French
The binding is by Custom Bookbinders